STEEP HOLM
LEGENDS
and HISTORY

RODNEY LEGG

Wincanton Press
National School, North Street, Wincanton, Somerset BA9 9AT

In memory of **Elizabeth Fowles** —
but for whose timely words Steep Holm
would never have become Allsop Island

Publishing details. First published 1993. Copyright © Rodney Legg 1993
Provisional permission for copying. This is intended as a source book for information
on Steep Holm and material may be quoted from it, providing the source is
acknowledged and mention is made of the work of the Kenneth Allsop Memorial Trust
in conserving the island. All other rights are reserved.
Printing credits. Typesetting input by Reg Ward at Holwell, Dorset, and output by
Wordstream Limited, Poole.
Illustrations processed by Fledermaus [the Strauss way — Zummerset spelling differs,
as other credit lines show] Printing Studio, 8 Buckland Road, Yeovil, Somerset.
Printed in Somerset by the Wincanton Print Company, at Wessex Way, Wincanton.
Telephone 0963 33643
Distribution. By Dorset Publishing Company from the Wincanton Press, National School,
North Street, Wincanton, Somerset BA9 9AT. Telephone 0963 32583.
International Standard Book Number. ISBN 0 948699 59 0

OPPOSITE. **Inspirational: international author John Fowles was not only the
prime instigator in the purchase of Steep Holm as a memorial for his
friend Kenneth Allsop — after wife and helpmate Elizabeth had swallowed
her doubts and given approval — but the couple then ensured the financial
support that brought the project to reality. That part of the story is the
third volume of this trilogy, entitled 'Allsop Island'. For now the present
book looks at distant history, inspired also by John Fowles who in 1977
helped Rodney Legg gather all that was then known about the Bristol
Channel island nature reserve for the first full-sized book to be devoted to
the 50-acre rock. Seen at his Belmont House home in Lyme Regis, Dorset.
Photographed by Colin Graham in 1972.**

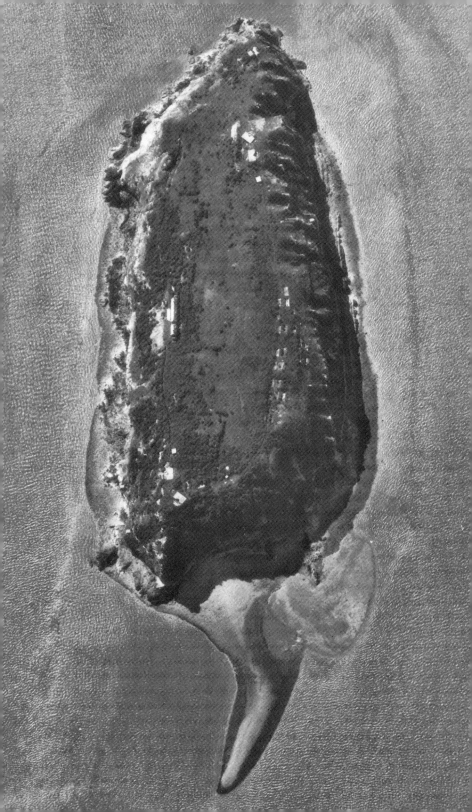

Contents

The Rock: Steep Holm, in mid Bristol Channel, halfway between England and Wales, showing dense patches of scrub and a scattering of Victorian Palmerstonian fortifications which were added to by the Royal Engineers in 1941 when the island was requisitioned for the Royal Artillery's Fixed Defences Severn. That part of the story is described in the second book of this series, 'Steep Holm at War'. Photographed at low water, when the pebble landing beach emerges from the sea and juts as a gooseneck towards Weston-super-Mare. The island expands at low tide from 50 to 63 acres. Patterns in the waves show currents and the darker patches are mud or turbidity. Seen from the east (bottom) with west at the top, south to the left, and north on the right. Photographed for the War Office in 1956.

Over the island: test-flight of Concorde's engine, replete with gull-catcher and mounted beneath an RAF Avro Vulcan bomber, as mentioned in the introduction to this book. Seen from the west, with the photographer's back to Steep Holm, looking towards the northern shore-line of Weston-super-Mare (Birnbeck Island, Anchor Head and the Marine Lake, at high tide) which is faintly discernible in the angle between the port wing and the tail. Photographed by Rolls-Royce in 1971.

Map: Steep Holm plus the Victorian 'e' which Chris Hall, the editor of The Countryman, still insists upon using. Ordnance Survey map, with north at the top. From a copy kindly provided by Dave Price and not requiring payment of a copyright fee as it is more than 50 years old. Surveyed in 1883 and revised in 1902.

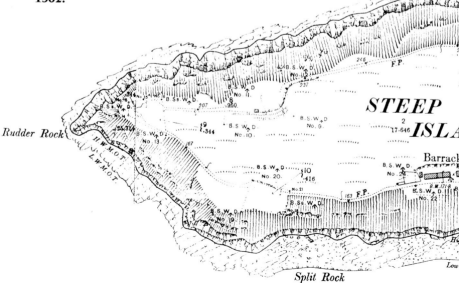

STEEP HOLME

(Wells Division)

Tower Rock

Calf Rock

Feet 100   0   500

Calm sea: a rare shot of Steep Holm in a state of balmy tranquillity, taken shortly before high tide with little showing of the pebbles at the landing beach (an inch from the left-hand rocky extremity). The darker shades on the left side represent the sycamore trees that have established a small wood on the eastern cliffs. The mound right of centre on the skyline protects the double Victorian barbettes of Laboratory Battery, constructed in 1866–68. The only other man-made lines are the 1941-built quay and boathouse beside the beach and the straight line of the concrete top of the contemporary 6-inch anti-ship gun emplacement of Garden Battery East (go along 65mm from the left-hand rocks, then 36mm up). Seen from the north-east. Photographed by Colin Graham in 1984.

OVERLEAF. **Space specks: the islands of Flat Holm (round in shape and off the upper, Welsh shore) and Steep Holm (egg-shaped and marginally closer to the right-hand English coast). They are seen from a satellite, passing over at 565 miles up, in a vertical shot with north at the top of the page — enabling direct comparison with a map. The islands lie in the neck of the Bristol Channel, between Lavernock Point in Wales and Brean Down which projects from Somerset as a promontory. The total width of the picture is 60 miles, from Swansea Bay (top left corner of the Channel) to Avonmouth (top right-hand corner). Darker shading indicates the mountains and uplands of South Wales, Exmoor and the Quantock Hills, and similarly the urban jungles of Port Talbot, Porthcawl, Barry, Cardiff and Newport (along the northern shore-line) and Bridgwater, Weston-super-Mare, Clevedon and Avonmouth (on the estuarine right-flank of the English side). Courtesy NASA, seen through a remote-sensing infra-red camera from Landsat-2 in May 1977.**

Cruel sea: island crossings are off the menu in conditions like this (above) but pick-ups are often accomplished in tricky circumstances. Occasionally, things go wrong, as this party of stranded visitors found when they were rescued by Weston inshore lifeboat (below) operating an emergency shuttle-service to the full-size Barry lifeboat which waited offshore (opposite) at dusk. Photographed by Rodney Legg in 1992.

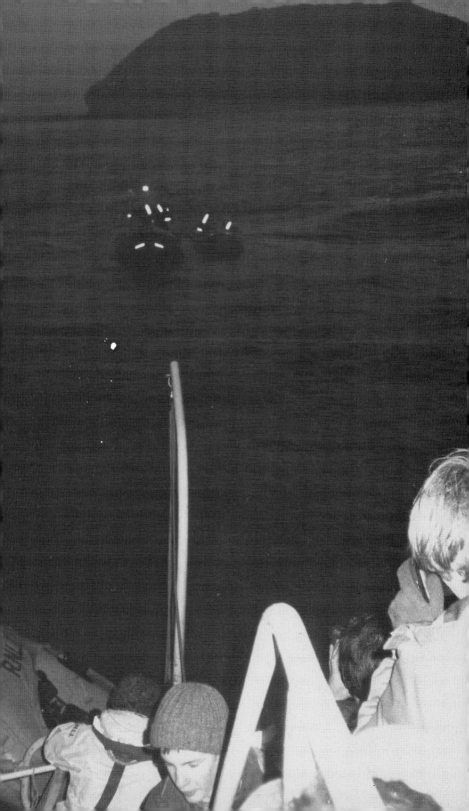

Speaking up for the environment: countryside campaigners Kenneth Allsop (opposite) and Rodney Legg (above and below). Steep Holm was bought as a nature reserve memorial to Allsop, who died in 1973, and Legg has been its warden since 1974. Allsop is pictured beside the sluices of his Milton Mill home in Dorset and Legg is seen on the island. Media photographs dating from 1971-89.

If once you have slept on an island
You'll never be quite the same.
You may look as you looked the day before,
And go by the same old name,
You may bustle about in street and shop,
You may sit at home and sew,
But you'll see blue water and wheeling gulls,
Wherever your feet may go.

Rachel Field [1894-1942]

Introduction

– to the Steep Holm trilogy:
the first book is *Steep Holm Legends and History*,
the second book is *Steep Holm at War*
and the third *Steep Holm – Allsop Island*

Steep Holm is not quite Lundy, though many mix up the names and locations of these English western isles. Much smaller, Steep Holm is the loaf-shaped rock that is seen end-on, in mid horizon, from the seafront at Weston-super-Mare. Further down the coast, from both Somerset and Wales, it appears much more menacing and dramatic, assuming the profile of the upturned hull of a great vessel, with the appropriately named semi-detached Rudder Rock pointing towards the Atlantic Ocean. Due west – a line that misses Lundy – there is no more dry ground until Newfoundland.

Our offshore outcrop of the Mendip Hills rises from the turbid and surging tidal waters of the Bristol Channel at latitude 51 degrees 20½ minutes north, longitude 3 degrees 6½ minutes west. The 256-feet high central plateau of Steep Holm is at Ordnance Survey map reference ST 229 607.

There is a magic and a mystery to the island that pre-dates its monastic ruins and has been enhanced by the discovery of Celtic carvings which indicate that there was a pagan shrine close to the site that became St Michael's Priory. Bridging the gap between the Celtic Island of the Severn Sea and the Augustinian monks is the legend of the "tread" of the phantom footsteps of Saint Gildas. Night on the island is full of sounds unfamiliar to mainlanders and their fitful sleep is conducive to a stream of ghostly claims that keep the story alive in the island visitors' book.

Not that Gildas has ever managed to wake me. I have been the warden of Steep Holm, or at least its absentee warden, since 1974 when the island was initially held on licence from the Honourable Mrs Ziki Robertson, now the eleventh Baroness Wharton, and then purchased, as a nature reserve memorial to Kenneth Allsop, the country's leading campaigning environmental broadcaster and journalist. Like Ken Allsop, I also feel compelled to write for a living, which has made me merely part-time warden, though I have used the opportunity to produce what will amount to a quarter of a million words about Steep

Holm when the current series of books is complete.

They will attempt to tell its story from geological time through to some of the hairy exploits that are the adventure of island going as our faithful team of boatmen attempt the double miracle of delivering us to this wind-blown rock and then retrieving us, as uneventfully as circumstances permit, at the end of the day.

As I write this, we are here for a little longer, with Jackie and Dave Price, from Bristol, looking after tabby-cat Salman and myself, plus miscellaneous day visitors, from Saturday through to Monday at an end of March Easter which coincides with big spring tides. Home is the Victorian Barracks block at the top of the southern cliffs, which is out of hearing of the sea and without an indoor view of it either.

Things are very different at the ruin of the former Inn on the eastern side of the island, where the sea ebbs and flows to lap the bottom of the wall twice a day. It has become the great project for the closing years of the twentieth century, to rebuild what will be a wardening depot and place to await the boat at the point where most of the dramas of arrival and pick-up take place, nearby on the pebble beach or beside it amid the rock pools.

There, between tides and bouts of Inn-building, Chris Maslen and Jenny Smith have taken on the sea and struggled to produce "a low-water exit" in the form of a stone jetty at the end of the jagged rocks.

The unexpected happens constantly on Steep Holm. On one extreme it is an eight-strong invasion by armed HM Customs and Excise officers from Avonmouth, in what turned out to be a fruitless search for smuggled drugs. The raid leads instead, through Gerry Sidney who runs an Army cadet unit, to the offer of a 40mm Bofors anti-aircraft gun of the type positioned here in the Second World War, as a military display piece.

At the other end of the spectrum, in nature's world, it is to be almost at the receiving end of superlative avian aerobatics, with a great whoosh of breaking air coming down at me as a Peregrine stoops immediately above my work-spot at the Inn. Speeds of 300 kilometres per hour have been ascribed to the bird but the proven maximum diving speed is much lower, at 132 kilometres per hour. Anyway, by the time I react the perpetrator has pulled out of the dive just above me and is heading seawards.

The cause of the excitement, a racing pigeon, has narrowly stayed off the menu, having swerved into the sycamore trees on the cliffs. Below, scattered up the path, are the stripped remains of others that were not so lucky.

I can receive something of a buzz from researching the island story when things eventually fall into place; such as Dave Price correcting a caption that it is too late for me to change in *Steep Holm at War*. We pace about outside the Barracks as he proves to me that an October 1941 picture of the massed ranks of 930 Port Construction and Repair Company of the Royal Engineers was not taken, as I had supposed, from the west end of the Nissen hut at the front of the Barracks. Photographer C. Maddison took his shot from immediately east of that point, before the hut was built.

Bob Moon then does likewise and finds a reference where I have unwittingly copied Victorian initials for the wrong kind of gun barrel. "M.L.R." stands for "Muzzle Loading Rifled" but is wrong for the 7-ton guns of Steep Holm as ours are "R.M.L." which stands for "Rifled Muzzle Loading".

In *Steep Holm – Allsop Island* I shall enthuse over the weekday aerobatics to which we are treated by the Royal Air Force, though here again I have one extra titbit that has come a little late in the day, courtesy John Pitfield eventually clipping through his stack of *Flight International*.

In 1971, RAF Vulcan delta-wing bomber XA903 made many fast sweeps from Filton down the Bristol Channel and into the South-Western Approaches before turning back on the same flight-path for home. At the controls was Rolls-Royce chief test pilot J. Pollitt and the Vulcan, one of the most graceful aircraft ever designed, was not quite as streamlined as her makers at Avro had intended.

For a start, running two-thirds of the way along her belly was an Olympus 593 engine which was box-shaped and as fat as her fuselage. The Vulcan was a flying test-bed for the intake icing trials of the engine that was being fitted in the new Anglo-French Concorde supersonic airliner.

Making the bomber particularly ungainly was an additional refinement that Filton engineers attached in order to deal with "the Steep Holm factor". Pilots had expressed concern at the enormous gullery through which the aircraft would have to pass. The solution was a "cow-catcher" mounted beneath the cockpit. This large, square, steel grill was angled backwards and supported from behind by two struts. Bird strikes fell clear of the air-intake of the Olympus engine which was a few feet behind.

Twenty years later, each evening, we experience the slight

tremor that ripples from Concorde's dying Atlantic boom and then see her coming home from New York, cruising at 30,000 feet on a line for Heathrow.

Next, to round off the day in the company of claret and cat, I can balance Salman's ground-watch by a view that is now at a premium in mainland Britain. From Steep Holm we not only see the lights of the Bristol Channel from the Severn Bridge to Ilfracombe but have a wide, clear sky, free of the bleaching effect caused by the glow of town street lighting. Not only are there the stars and occasional meteor showers but the game that requires the most attention, to manage a decent score, is to spot the satellites crossing the sky. They are still illuminated for a couple of hours after the sun has set on us.

I hope that from this trilogy it will be apparent that the island is the place where I can find myself at my happiest. To an extent it depends on what young friends turn up to brighten my day. It requires Jenny Smith for a decent dose of black humour. "Cor, she's hard," says one of the lads, Martin Payne from Bristol's Hartcliffe estate, in admiration at her capacity to lift and carry hundredweight bags of cement as if in zero gravity. For most of the time, however, hassles of wardening preclude escapism and problems imported from the mainland remain part of life's baggage.

Tomorrow is not only another day but quite likely a different mood, as will be seen when I scribble out an introduction to cover the other couple of books.

R.L.

The Barracks, Steep Holm
County of Avon (detached)   Easter Sunday, 30 iii 91

Giant of Gorm

History, for Steep Holm, begins with legend as it does in all lands. There is a mythical monster in the form of the Giant of Gorm. He fights with Vincent, the Lord of Avon, for the possession of the Avon Gorge. "Vincent, however, was victor, for Gorm tripped in his flight like Enceladus," writes Charles Henry Poole in his 1877 collection of *The Customs, Superstitions, and Legends of the County of Somerset*. The allusion to Enceladus comes from Virgil's *Aeneid*. The giant Enceladus was flying across the Mediterranean when Athene, the goddess of the sky, picked up Sicily and threw the island at him.

As for Gorm, or Goram as he is called at Blaise Castle where there is a Giant Goram's Chair, he fell flat in the Bristol Channel and drowned, his bones forming the islands of Steep Holm and Flat Holm and the headland of Brean Down. Earlier, in his clumsy striding across the West Country, he is said to have created Maes Knoll – an outcrop at Whitchurch, south of Bristol – when the earth slipped off his spade. The embellishment to that story is that as the gormless colossus leaned on to his spade to contemplate matters it sank into the ground and created the long deep-cut ditch known as Wansdyke.

Thus were the larger ancient monuments, from time out of mind, explained away by the country people, and the story also accounted for the odd island or two. It was left to the pseudo-historians, primarily Geoffrey of Monmouth [?1100-54] in his *Historia Britonum*, to assume a chronology that traced the descent of British princes from the Trojans. Vincent was claimed to be the Romanised name of a Celtic chieftain, a leader of the Belgae, who had displaced the Gauls to become the most formidable of the tribes on the seaboards of both sides of the English Channel. As Gorm's name sank without trace, Vincent's was applied to the rocks beside the Clifton suspension bridge.

OPPOSITE. **Homeward-bound: gulls silhouetted in the sunset, to a backdrop of their Steep Holm home. 'Holm' is the Norse word for an estuarine island and this evocative picture is our holm as it was experienced by boatmen for centuries. Those words are past-tense as gull numbers have since crashed from thousands to hundreds, reduced by avian botulism. This is caused by clostridium, the pathogenic bacterium which has become common in summertime, developing when household rubbish putrifies in the anaerobic conditions of sealed plastic bin-liners that have been left out in the sun. Steep Holm is seen from the east. Photographed by Colin Graham in 1984.**

21

Geology, fossils, ores

Superficially, the island's geology has apparent uniformity. It is around 330 milllion years old, of grey Carboniferous Limestone, and was laid down in early Carboniferous times as billions of tiny particles derived from the breaking up of shells decaying on a sea bottom that was slowly subsiding at the time of its deposition. The age of the Carboniferous period was first estimated in the early twentieth century, by extrapolating the rates of radioactive decay in the metallic element uranium. Arthur Holmes gives the 330 million years date in *The Age of the Earth*, first published in 1913 and revised in 1927. The rock itself is of calcium carbonate ($CaCO_3$; the molecules each comprise one atom of calcium, one of carbon and three of oxygen). There are also thin bands of clay, sandy matter, and metallic ores such as haematite (red iron oxide, Fe_2O_3).

These mineral veins include galena (lead ore; blue-grey cubic crystals of lead sulphide, PbS) and are of secondary origin. They came into the layers of limestone from external sources, after it had consolidated. Galena was first smelted on the Mendip Hills for lead and silver in Roman times and at intervals up to the late nineteenth century.

Joints in the island's rock were caused by shrinkage (tension), and by compressional pressures.

In many places there are visible fossils, the remains of which are now marked by white mineral calcite. You can see them the moment you step up off the beach, in the outcrop immediately above you to the left. There geologist Rod Simm, from Solihull, pointed out to me the sections of *Bellerophon* (a primitive snail which has a whirl similar to that of some present-day pond snails), brachiopods (early sea-shells) and the cross sections and longitudinal stems of sea-lilies or crinoids (sedentary relations of the present-day sea urchins and starfish). Corals also occur and these fossiliferous beds can be traced laterally along the layers.

It is pointless trying to hammer away at these fossils, because they cannot be detached by chipping, and the effort would be better employed in searching the beach for a trasportable specimen that is exposed in a pebble. My examples of *Paleosmilia murchisoni*, solitary, non-reef forming Carboniferous corals about two inches across, were picked up on the scree slopes.

"Note the small fault in the cliff-face above the path at the Inn," Simm told me. "It can be seen as a more steeply sloping line than the rock layers, but still tilting to the south. The rocks dip between 20 degrees and 40 degrees south."

Even that is a simplification. By matching the beds on either side of the fault one can see that the beds above the fault have been pushed from the south over the underlying beds, which means that it is a thrust fault.

The topography of Britain during the formation of Steep Holm was that of a large mass of land lying across North Wales and Central England, called St George's Land by geologists, which was flanked to the south by clear shallow tropical shelf seas like the present-day Bahamas. The present-day sites of Cardiff and Bristol docks were, at times during the period, shallow lagoons floored with lime-mud. At other times in deeper, bluer water the last relics of the Devonian period's great armoured fish swam slowly through the forests of sea-lilies and coral reefs over the place where Steep Holm would eventually stand in the murky, cold waters of today's Bristol Channel.

At the time of the slow depositing of the sediments that became Steep Holm rock strata the area was under the sea. The general character of the organisms making up the rock is remarkably consistent throughout the several thousand feet of sediment which make up the Carboniferous Limestone – although there are suffecient differences for the strata to be separated into thinner rock units or formations. It seems the rock was all laid down in shallow water, zero to 300 feet or so, although in theory the water should get shallower as the rock is deposited. This apparent inconsistency is explained by the gradual sinking of a large area of western Europe at the same time as the sediment was accumulating.

The island beds belong to the middle part of the Carboniferous Limestone and Gilbert Green of the British Geological Survey (BGS), during the official 6-inch to the mile survey in the mid-1970s, showed that 300 feet of strata, subdivided into fan formations, are present.

It is the position of Steep Holm that gives the island particular geological significance, mentioned by the Nature Conservancy as supporting evidence for the listing of the island as a place of special scientific interest. The island lies five or six miles from Weston-super-Mare and a similar distance from Lavernock Point, Wales, but it is only three-and-a-half miles from another headland of Mendip limestone, Brean Down in Somerset.

Professor Emeritus J.G.C. Anderson, formerly head of the geology department at University College, Cardiff, cautioned me against the general assumption by non-geologists that Steep Holm is simply an offshoot of the Mendips. He pointed out that "the relationship between the Carboniferous rocks of the north side of the Bristol Channel and those on the south side is still a matter of considerable doubt and controversy". The links above the tide-line are the islands of Steep Holm, Flat Holm and Denny. Of these Professor Anderson says, "Steep Holm is the most significant" and he spoke against any development which might cover or spoil the island's geological exposures, adding that future access "to study its geology is of considerable importance".

There is a major difference between Brean Down and Steep Holm. On Brean Down the strata slope or dip is at about 30 degrees to the north, whereas beside the beach at Steep Holm the tilting or dip is in the other direction, at about 30 degrees to the south.

Gilbert Green explained to me that the significance of this difference is that when the rocks are traced from north to south across Steep Holm they are found to be getting older. The reverse holds for Brean Down. It follows that one cannot be a direct continuation of the other – they do not 'fit'.

I tried to summarise the landforms of the island in *The Steep Holm Guide*, in a paragraph so terse that it defies further condensation:

"48.87 acres above high-tide, but expanding to 63.26 acres at mean low water. Elliptical, 825 metres (east to west) by 315 metres (north to south) extending to 1,230 metres by 360 metres at low tide when the sea uncovers a long goose-neck spit of shingle off the east landing beach and a rocky shelf around the rest of the island. Several phreatic caves, in formerly submerged limestone, and 'false caves' – fissures and blow-holes – caused by wave action. Rock-arches at Rudder Rock. The island has precipitous northern cliffs and a southern side angled more gently, at about 30 degrees, with scree slopes between the rocky outcrops. The top of the island is a domed plateau, rising to 78 metres."

Gilbert Green comments: "This account closely relates to the geological structure of the island. The elliptical slope elongated in an E.N.E.-W.S.W. direction is directly due to the E.N.E.-W.S.W. grain or strike of the rocks (the strike is a horizontal plane measured at right angles to the dip). The more gently angled southern side of the island corresponds to ruling dips of around 20 degrees to the S.S.E. The precipitous northern cliffs correspond to a sharp upturn of the strata in the northern quarter of the island to about 75 degrees. This upturn occurs along a hinge line that follows the grain of the rocks across the island between Monks' Well at the eastern end and south of Rudder Rock at the western end."

The most dramatic geological feature visible on the island itself is in the second cove north-west of the Inn. Here the inclined strata from the beach, on which the Inn is also built, suddenly turn downwards and then upwards in a dramatic fold. The rocks are mainly greyish-white and more or less oolitic limestone.

This major fold, first pointed out to me by Rod Simm, is beneath the Monks' Well and clearly visible on the vertical cliff-face, "just to the left of a hollow in the cliffs at about ten feet off the shingle". In making the transition from 30 degrees to 75 degrees the limestone beds turn first into a tight anticlinal fold with a very steep northerly dip along the hinge line, then are vertical. Fractures at its core indicate that the fold axial plane then dips to the south at about 75 degrees.

More impressive, however, are the lower cliffs around Split Rock but these can only be viewed from offshore. Gilbert Green has studied the island in the greatest depth and carried out more visits than any other geologist. He enthused at the sight of Split Rock from the boat: "Here the rocks are contorted and the pressures were so intense that the limestone has behaved like extruded toothpaste, which is most unusual for Carboniferous Limestone."

Split Rock is also remarkable beneath the water. The £700,000 seabed survey carried out for the Department of Energy and Severn Tidal Power Group in 1987 plotted, by marine seismic reflections from a boat-towed boomer to hydrophones following behind, several previously unknown pot-holes on the seabed off Split Rock. All were filled with sand and gravel and so do not figure on the Admiralty chart. The surprise for the geeologists was that one is 60 metres deep and seems to be part of a collapsed cave system. They reported: "As the sea level rose again after the last Ice Age these channels and depressions subsequently became filled with sand, gravel, cobbles and boulders. Up to 40 metres of sediments have been encountered in some places."

That sums up the origins and fabric of the island. It would, according to Professor Arthur Holmes, have developed into its present insular form about 180,000,000 years ago. Subsequent changes in sea level would have taken it under the water and buried it under sediment, and at other times made it an island, and then an inland cliff. It was about 65,000,000 years ago that there was a general uplift of the earth's crust in the area that now contains the British Isles.

The upper Bristol Channel area was mostly land in the period about 30,000,000 years ago when the collision of the earth's tectonic plates caused the upswelling of major mountain ranges. The Bristol Channel emerged from this with the basic features it has today and subsequently Steep Holm would be surrounded by the sea during the inter-glacial periods and become part of the land during the glaciations. One of the warmings of climate unlocked so much of the polar ice that the sea rose eighty feet above its present levels, up the sides of the island, to leave a raised-beach strand-line of sea worn caves, pebbles and quantities of blown sand. The caves, being the creation of erosion rather than geology, deserve their own section.

As for the "mainstream" geology, the work of Gilbert Green has shown that the Steep Holm landforms are only dismissed as simple by those who have failed to notice or understand them.

Landform geology: superbly twisted and crumpled strata exposed above rock-pools at the north-east corner of the island. Seen from the north. Photographed by Colin Graham in 1975.

OPPOSITE. Sea-cut arches: looking inside Rudder Rock, which is topped by a 1941-built searchlight post. Seen from the south. Photographed by John Pitfield in 1990.

Cavernous: caves accessible only at low-tide, and then by wading, at the north-eastern corner of the island (above) plus the exposed back end of a cave system broken into by the sea (below). Seen from the east (above) and north (below). Photographed by Colin Graham in 1976.

Rock-arches and caves

Sea-cut rock-arches, through which it is possible to walk at extreme low tide, form the western tip of the island and give it the name Rudder Rock. The ancient structural features of the island show that many millions of years ago the sea was working away at a much higher level. A line of mural and columnar tors, with other doorway-type structures, are visible from the clifftop to the east of Summit Battery. Midway down that cliff the sea has left a wave-cut platform, now largely filled and turned into a slope by accumulating scree and earth, but still with some beach pebbles. Rising from it is a vertical cliff-face with eroded cavities of varying sizes.

On the south-east corner of the island, between the sea-level Calf Rock and the base of the two hundred foot Tower Rock outcrop, there is an area at the high tide mark which displays solution sculpture of the stone.

The caves, on the ancient sea-levels on the sides of the island, and those down in its present inter-tidal zone, provide the most fascinating aspect of Steep Holm geology for the layman. The higher caves are now dry and no longer growing. Those on the shore, however, are below the island's water-table and very much alive. Spring-water seeping from phreatic passages causes calcareous deposits and stalactites, though not stalagmites as they cannot grow because the floors are too often washed out by the sea. Cross-rifts and other enlargements form where different solutions meet.

Hall Cave, in the north corner of the second cove around from the Inn, at the north-east side of the island, is a typical smoothly-rounded cavity, 40 feet deep, 20 feet wide and 18 feet high. At the far end it has a small phreatic bell – a hemispherical instrusion into the rear wall. The entrance to Hall Cave is through a knee-deep tide pool ten feet across, closely overhung by an arch of rock, and I'm too nervous to cross this in swimming trunks as I once saw a huge conger eel that had been caught nearby.

The insidious danger of venturing into Hall Cave is that you can be cut off by the rising tide which rapidly fills the cove outside. To add to the sensation of impending doom, anyone foolish enough to disregard the tides or the state of the water – in a north-easterly gale the sea can pile waves into this cave even at theoretical low-tide – there is an accompanying eerie music. Colin Rogers, a Mendip caver, told me about an echoing death-knell that comes from outside: "A nearby blow-hole in the cliffs produces an awesome booming sound in the chamber at certain states of the tide."

Only a few feet to the south, in Jubilee Cave, there is a more advanced chamber. It is similar to Hall Cave in size, but higher as rocks have broken away from the roof where cracks have opened, giving it the look of jagged confusion rather than rounded conformity. These fractures have been caused by nature's acid rain, a weak solution of carbonic acid – atmospheric carbon dioxide dissolved in rainwater – which drips through the porous rock. Below these joints and cracks there are piles of rubble. Obscure passages lead into a variety of cave formations. Here Colin Rogers found a pile of old bat droppings in February 1975. The cave has deposits of red ochre, stalactite straws and flowstone, on which there is some microflora.

The greatest interest in Hall and Jubilee caves is not inside but outside. The cove was once underground and formed the back part of a huge cave system. The sea broke through into this ancient cave and caused its collapse, with now only the back cavities of Hall Cave and Jubilee Cave surviving inside the cliff. Rogers writes: "Features around the bay immediately in front of these two caves and their tide pools indicate they once belonged to one, much larger, cave. A magnificent arching promontory of rock, opposite Hall Cave, appears to have been the back wall of a chamber. Many phreatic pockets around the area support this impression. The two existing caves are only back-chambers of the main cave. The floor of the bay is criss-crossed with haematite and galena veins. To the west there are several blow-holes that throw water-spouts when the sea is rough."

Neither cave, however, equates with Francis Knight's 1902 description in *The Sea-board of Mendip* where he describes a massive chamber named Church Cave: "On the north side of Steep Holm there is a cave running deep into the island. It is difficult of access and although above high-water, can only be reached at low tide. It was visited about 1880 by two men from Weston, who brought away a number of stalactites of great size and beauty. They also saw bats in great masses hanging from the roof. The explorers crawled through a narrow passage into a much more spacious chamber beyond. From the roof of this hung many fine stalactites, and the floor was covered with a sheet of water."

I have puzzled over this description for several years. There was no known contender on the north side of the island at the time I compiled *Steep Holm – a case history in the study of evolution*, in 1978, and I tentatively suggested that this Church Cave might lie beyond Window Cave on the south side of the island. This is so-called because it is a hole in the rock-face which one can climb into and use as a window on the sea. It lies between Reservoir Cavity and Split Rock. There is the potential for some-thing more at the back because a bedding plane or fault runs from the south-west (where it is open to the sea) to the north-east, and continues for 70 feet to a salt-water rock-pool that is 30 feet long. The end lies beyond my chimneying abilities.

Then, in 1979 on a walk around the island tide-line, on one of several occasions when I heard on the radio that we were experiencing the "lowest tides of the century", I spotted a great cleft rising into the northern rocks between Summit Battery and Rudder Rock. Its slippery slope is covered with flowstone and I therefore dubbed it White Cave. This hole also proved too much for my climbing expertise and I slithered down to a minor bruising.

So there are currently two contenders for the Church Cave search. It is time that this form of study progressed from an explorative to a scientific level. While investigations in 1933, 1935, 1956, 1963 and 1975 added some knowledge of the island's underground it seemed to be reaching the stage where each new group was re-finding the carbide writings of its prede-cessors. The fun had to stop when an accident in 1975 left its victim hanging for hours at the end of a rope and forced the island's management committee to curb the island's freedom to potholers. The Kenneth Allsop Memorial Trust announced that it had forbidden all future use of the island for general caving and rock climbing. This is owing to the obvious difficulties of coping in an emergency, and the problem with the tidal caves is that they are likely to be cut off by the sea before help arrives.

As for the cliffside caves even these are inaccessible. Five Johns' Cave is a massive resurgence, possibly the back-wall of another large cave that has been captured by the sea, about fifty yards west of Hall Cave and some thirty-five feet above the shore. It is in a precipitous wall of rock – here, at least, the bats are still undisturbed.

Tree Cave is a large, dry opening halfway up the cliff, immediately above the former raised beach to the north-west of Laboratory Battery. It is twenty-five feet high with an opening at the top and an elder tree growing from the floor. Here at the bottom there is an arch which opens as a window on the sea with a fine view of Flat Holm. Not that I am ever likely to see it again. Between 1974 and 1984 the raised beach beneath the cave had become an erased beach. Chris Maslen strode on ahead, oblivious to the loose stones he was sending down into the water, and I held Jenny Smith's hand as we inched around the base of precipitous outcrops and then crawled on our knees back on to the top of the island.

Further to the west, accessible but unimpressive, is Steps Cave. This is just above the searchlight post at the bottom of 208 Steps. It is a small phreatic cavity in an haematite vein, less than ten feet deep, and its main interest is an apparently undisturbed floor which may contain dateable material.

A similar boring cavity, level with the beach wall, goes into the eastern cliff beside the lower section of path from the Boathouse to the Inn. It is called Hole Passage, which sums up what it has to offer. It is at least thirty feet deep but does not seem to lead to anything other than a five-foot wide chamber.

Raven's Nest Cave, on the north face of Tower Rock, is a smaller than average cave, no more than three feet deep, and is a mid-cliff phreatic fissure. As with the others it is now dry, and as for the ravens, they have moved westwards to the other side of South Landing.

Here is Reservoir Cavity, a small cave in a haematite vein, just above the high-water mark. It was dammed by the War Department in 1866 to hold fresh water that trickles from above. On the cliff-edge a winching point was built, with grooves in its seaward face for the control of the ropes, and this was the Water Haul for the island's drinking water until the Barracks Reservoir was operational.

Above the South Landing, to the south of the eastern of the island's three wartime generator houses, lies Parsons Cave. It made its debut into print in comparatively recent times, reported by Stan and Joan Rendell in the issue of the Steep Holm Magazine for 1985, which was a problem year for the apostrophe as they call it Parson's (sic) Cave "partly in recognition of its discoverer" Tony Parsons, but also because of the "Brandy for the Parson" line in Rudyard Kipling's *A Smuggler's Song*. If named for the person it should be Parsons' Cave and if for the tippling clergyman it is Parson's Cave.

The smuggling connection came about because it was walled-up, to make a hideaway, and it will therefore be mentioned later in the island's smuggling history. As for the hole, it is dry with an arched roof two metres high and 2.5 metres deep. The ground outside is a flat shelf that extends to the back of the dry cave. Either side there is a vertical ivy-covered cliff with a companion Little Cave two metres to the east. This cave is two metres wide, 1.5 metres high and two metres deep.

Their ledge is at about 185 feet above the present sea-level and is the highest of the cliff-edge cave systems. In fact even the domed top of the island has traces of water-caused deposits from the collapsed remains of overlying beds.

A wide area around the Ordnance Survey's instrument pillar is almost level at 256 feet. The path to the north of it, between Summit Battery and Laboratory Battery, runs consistently at about the 238 feet contour. The minimal degree of slope across the top of the island is insufficient to allow run-off rainfall to cause soil-loss, and the limestone tends to act like a sponge. Soil accumulates rather than being lost, and wind erosion does not seem to be a problem even on the exposed top of the island. Indeed after one south-easterly gale I noticed a minute drifting of fine sand across the paths. It had come from the great beaches and dunes of Bleadon and Brean.

Only sand particles of less than 0.0039 inch diameter can be held in suspension by the wind, but these can be carried great distances, sometimes from the eastern Sahara. This, happening locally with a hundred times the quantities, is the clue to the surface geology of Brean Down, where large areas of the limestone promontory are covered by deep deposits of blown sand. Much of the vegetation has its roots in this acid layer. Although this is unlikely to be a factor of consequence on Steep Holm it is a reminder that coastal geology is not always as clear cut as it appears.

In places on the high plateau the soil is between six inches and a foot in depth. It is thin and red, stained by the iron from veins in the rock, and in 1974 we found a fragment of stalactite in a rabbit hole. The following year, between the Ordnance Survey pillar and Laboratory Battery, a caving group from Locking RAF station dug out that burrow in the interests of science. Numerous fragments of stalactite were found – enough to show, there at least, that extensive debris from crushed stalactite formations mark the site of a former cave system.

We had hoped to stumble into a shaft. Hell's Hole – the location of which is now lost – was a "bottomless" pothole on the top of the island that has become part of Steep Holm memories of the Harris family of Victorian innkeepers.

Cavemen and Mesolithic hunters

Steep Holm would have looked a fantastic place in 10,000 BC. The southern edge of the northern polar ice-cap was in retreat and the melt-waters of Pleistocene ice sheets were gushing down the rocky channel between the headlands of Steep Holm and Flat Holm. I say headlands, rather than islands, because the tundra-people of Mendip could walk from Brean Down to Steep Holm.

Even now the waters of the Bristol Channel are not generally deep. The exception is a trough half-a-mile north-west of Rudder Rock, at 19 fathoms (114 feet), which was an offshoot from the Ice Age river-bed of the River Severn. I think that this hole is the collapsed remains of the caverns of a huge cave system. The Severn Ice-Age river bed is a mile-and-a-half north of the island and is some 12 fathoms (72 feet) below present low-tide levels.

On the other side of that trench, 5,000 feet south-west of Flat Holm, the seabed is only three fathoms, with a wreck known as the Mackenzie Shoal. The greatest depth between Steep Holm and Weston-super-Mare is 12 fathoms (72 feet) though there is only two fathoms of water (12 feet) under the site of the pre-1988 South Patches Buoy, a mile-and-a-half east of the island, at low tide.

Because of the constant churning of huge tides the Bristol Channel always appears muddy but *The Geology of the Severn Barrage Area*, a paper produced by the Institute of Geological Studies, shows that much of the estuary between Lavernock Point and Brean Down has exposed bedrock on the seabed.

North-east of Flat Holm there are great areas of shallows, from which the gritty Holm sand is now dredged by a fleet of ships operating out of Bridgwater, and that island was connected to the Welsh shore. To the west of Rudder Rock the Severn captured the melting glaciers of the Brecon Beacons, surging down the River Taff, for their next confluence – with the sea.

Permafrost still gripped the Black Mountains, which were then a white backdrop to the Steep Holm view. By 9,000 BC the gradual warming of the climate was drawing man westwards and northwards from the Mendip caves and enabling him to live in outdoor shelters. Summertime on the southern shores of the Severn estuary would have been much like it is experienced in Greenland today. The alpine flora has a quick and colourful burst into life, the seals have their pups, and fauna includes the larger predators – those man has made extinct since the detachment from Europe at the Straits of Dover – namely the bear, the beaver and the wolf. There were herds of reindeer and the summertime presence of the wild boar, extending its range as scrubland and then woodland advanced northward.

One of the Steep Holm caves has yielded relics of prehistoric caveman. It could only have been through human activity that the vertebrae of a red deer came to be in Five Johns' Cave which is totally inaccessible except by climbers using ropes. Ray Coles entered it on the RAF Locking caving expedition of 1975 and found the bones, later authenticated by Woodspring Museum, lying in undisturbed ancient debris that half filled the circular cavity.

Man returned to Steep Holm between 8,000 and 6,000 BC in the period we know as the Mesolithic, which was a hunter-gatherer lifestyle. As it became surrounded by the estuary the shrinking island would have concentrated the seals and sea-birds on the rocks and inaccessible cliffs. The rising waters may have cut-off and stranded a family or two of man on the newly detached Steep Holm. Its size at first would have been several hundred acres with great tongues of rock-pools and sandbanks extending from the island at low tide. This would have been a highly desirable micro-habitat given that it had security from other human beings, before the general use of dug-out canoes and then coracles, and the problem of competition from nature's predators could be kept to a minimum.

Sea-food and sea-birds would have supplemented the seal-meat diet. Even today, on the Vestmannaejar off Iceland, puffin and black-backed gulls are smoked during the breeding season for all-year consumption. Agriculture and horticulture were still unknown; indeed unnecessary because the dramatic change in the climate would have been increasing the biomass yearly. The amount of material in the food chain was rising all the time as the flora went through its slow transition from tundra to climax woodland. It was only at the last stage, the forest canopy, that the food supply would level off and the expansion in human numbers give rise to dependence upon farming.

That Mesolithic man walked Steep Holm is now beyond doubt. A few worked microlith flints – a tool imported from the chalk downs of Wessex – were found during the Priory excavations of 1977-92. They may also have produced roughly-shaped home-made tools, like the chert picks found at Portland Bill in Dorset, though as yet no larger implement has been discovered on the island.

Neolithic visitors

Neolithic man brought agriculture and grave-architecture to Britain at the end of the Mesolithic period, or at least that was what was assumed until Colin Renfrew's *Before Civilisation*, published in 1973, pointed out the implications of the re-calibration of radio carbon dating upon the generally accepted archaeological chronologies. The megalithic buildings, it had been previously thought, had sailed into Ireland and Britain from the Iberian peninsula, but Renfrew shows that the passage graves of northern France pre-date the megaliths and dolmens of Portugal by a thousand years and that the movements were in the opposite direction. Dated to 4,300 BC the megalithic chamber tombs are older than the Pyramids and are the "earliest stone monuments in the world".

Regretfully, Steep Holm does not have its cromlech nor any standing stone, but in the third millennium BC the island was visited by Neolithic man. They came, perhaps, for fish and eggs, or young birds, or possibly by complete accident, as mariners in a storm have found themselves unexpectedly landing on islands the world over.

Either way they would have carried their tools, which were still mainly flints in this pre-metal era, and these were reaching a degree of sophistication with wooden and leather mountings and straps. Those the archaeological team has recovered so far from the island are of the common scraper type, four being found in the Priory excavations of 1977-92, though one is a palm-sized implement.

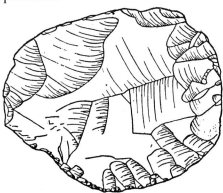

Flint scraper: typical of the Wessex downland-type implements that are found on Steep Holm, this discoidal flint knife being from near Old King Barrows, Amesbury. Drawn for Wiltshire Archaeological Society in 1964.

Bluestones passed by

The first great cargo of the western world passed by Steep Holm in about 1,900 BC. It was a feat of navigation and human endeavour that can seldom have been matched since, given the relatively frail nature of the craft that were available, and its achievement is part of the enigma of Stonehenge. Unless, that is, its bluestones were not man-moved at all but ice-flow erratics from 400,000 BC. For the present, however, the general received wisdom is that they were brought from Wales by Bronze Age man.

Preseli Mountain, in Pembrokeshire, was sacred – there can be no other reasonable explanation for what took place – and blocks of stone quarried there were shipped the ninety miles from Milford Haven to the upper waters of the Bristol Channel off Steep Holm. From here they were manoeuvred inland via the river systems; in all probability being taken further up the estuary and then floated to the Wiltshire end of the Avon valley, being hauled from there via Westbury and then rafted down the River Wylye to make the left turn into the other River Avon at Salisbury. Alternatively, they may have sailed up the River Brue from the inundated Somerset Levels and had the drag into the Wylye over the line of hills at Longleat.

If they had taken the third "possible" route, around Lands End, they would have been mad – and anyway fragments of this stone found in Wiltshire burial mounds suggest there had indeed been an overland route. The stones of Stonehenge that are from Preseli are not the really huge sarsens of the main monument but the lesser alignments of spotted dolerite, "bluestones" as they are called, inside. The remains of twenty-nine have been found but only six are still standing more or less intact. They had formed a circle of uprights inside which there is a horseshoe of similar uprights open at the north-east (from its northern extremity across to the eastern extremity) towards the rising midsummer sun. In all there must have been about forty bluestones originally.

The stones are dull and grey except after rain when they do shine blue. There is a tendency towards them acquiring a polish, both naturally and from human touch, and in three cases they are unspotted. If fractured, some appear coarse-grained and crystalline, with the general speckling and glinting being clearly caused by nodules of felspar that range in size from a grain to a pea. Others are of rhyolite, a flinty blue-grey volcanic lava, and others still are a soft olive-green volcanic ash. All are igneous and those of the ash-type would have been easily removed in later times.

This stone occurs across only a square mile of the far west of Wales and the hypothesis that it could have been spread around the West Country by glaciation has been discounted by geologists. In collecting fanciful theories for my book on the *Stonehenge Antiquaries* I had hoped to come across some suggestions as to why Preseli Mountain was regarded with such awe that man felt the need to transport its stone nearly two hundred miles (it is 135 miles as the crow flies, but that option wasn't open to them). There is no suitably bizarre theory, mainly because the stone was not identified with Preseli until 1923, so you just have my opinion – that the sun sets into Carn Meini and Foel Trigarn, the eastern end of the range, for the peoples of a great area of Dyfed and it is the last fling of the Cambrian Mountains before St David's Channel. That's my view – the sun sleeps in Preseli Mountain and its east-facing slopes welcome its return in the morning.

That thought came to me when I was listening on the radio to the beliefs of the Australian aborigines. "The sun will rise again," one of them said. There was an empathy with nature that is lost by religions as they proceed into theology. It is sad to think of the rag-bag of beliefs we have given them in exchange.

The question of the Stonehenge bluestones and their transit beside Steep Holm was studied by Cardiff dentist Wystan Peach in the mid-1970s. He even hired a helicopter to search for fragments that might have dropped off en route. I was able to provide details of some alien blue-stones in the island, one or two of which appear in the western walling of the Priory, but these are still in situ and the general geological opinion is that they are blue lias. On the other hand I have noticed that they seem to have suffered minimal weathering since exposure in about 1977.

My first opinion was that they are the so-called Keinton marble, a hard-wearing blue-grey stone from Keinton Mandeville on the Fosse Way, north of Ilchester, that takes a polish and was used for flagstones all over south Somerset.

I told Mr Peach that I doubted if the early navigators would have risked using Steep Holm as anything other than an entirely involuntary stopping point. The tides are hostile and the conditions hazardous for any boatman who is not au fait with the changing shape of the island's shingle spit. No one is going to risk that with a small craft that is overloaded with stone blocks weighing upwards of a ton.

John Fowles and I scoured the beach for sea-worn chunks of bluestone. We used to do that each time our boat for home was late and we agreed that if we should ever find any it would be because there had been a disaster in antiquity.

I have similar reservations about an alleged piece of Neolithic bowl which Leo Harrison Matthews and a group of excavators from Bristol Naturalists' Society found when they dug inside the east end of the Priory ruin in 1938. "The pottery is very mixed," he wrote, "the oldest fragment being part of the foot of a neolithic bowl." Given that he mistook a mediaeval memorial stone for a coffin lid, I am doubtful about his dating. The excavation carried out in the Priory site by Stan and Joan Rendell in 1977-92 has accumulated 3,000 potsherds, much of it coarseware including pieces of mediaeval pottery that had lost their glaze, but nothing is pre-Roman.

Efforts were made in the late 1970s to find the reputedly Neolithic discovery but all the material appears to have been taken to Bristol and lost.

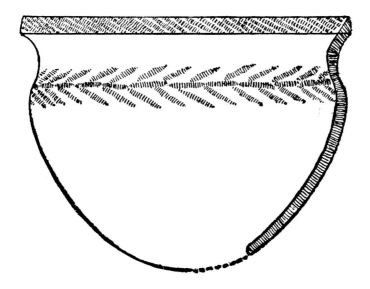

Neolithic bowl: that from Rowberrow Cavern in the Mendip Hills, shown here a little smaller than actual size, is the closest parallel in terms of round-bottom design and geographical proximity to the fragment that Harrison Matthews recalled from Steep Holm. Drawn by Bristol Spelaeological Society in the 1920s.

Little head: Leo Harrison Matthews's Celtic head of the Roman period, enlarged from thumb-size reality to show the incredible detail carved in-the-round and of totally Celtic design. Photographed by Barry Cousens in 1992.

Celtic island
of the Severn Sea

The dedication of the mediaeval Steep Holm Priory is circumstantial evidence for earlier Celtic connections. Churches to St Michael, archangel of the armies of heaven, are not only associated with high places but frequently coincide with those where evidence of pre-Christian religions has been found. Unusually, such churches sometimes have their graveyards on the north side – as on Steep Holm – which indicates the continuity of a burial ground from pagan times. Standing in such churchyards and looking east, the church is then to your right, in the southerly position associated with St Michael and a symbolic block between the light of God from that direction and the darkness of the devil to the north.

The island has produced two religious cult objects from pagan times. First to be found, of not much more than thumb-nail size, was a tiny head picked up by Leo Harrison Matthews in the 1930s in a heap of stones to the north of the Priory ruins.

Dr Matthews posted it to me from Suffolk after I had sent him a complimentary copy of our *Steep Holm* book in 1978. I telephoned him and was told it was a personal thank-you, the head having been retained among a collection of island souvenirs: "Which as it turns out was the best thing for the objects, given that all the material that went into museums has now been lost."

He described the spot where it was found as "a sort of cairn of displaced or collapsed walling" between the Priory and Tombstone Battery, "pretty obvious and only a few feet from the path at the top of the island". I explained that the spot was now far from visible, having been subjected to massive disturbance in 1941 when a railhead and Nissen huts were constructed beside it. It has become engulfed in privet scrub.

The head is of carboniferous limestone that is grey at the top, changing through to pink and then white, with crystals at the bottom. It represents a male head, carved in the round, with a classic wedge-shaped nose and limed hair which zig-zags down the back. The basic shape is triangular, but in a three dimensional sense rather than in relief. The stone must have been very hard to carve and all the more skill would have been needed because of its minuscule size.

This head makes its debut in print in this book. Meanwhile,

however, a second would be picked up, by Terry Gore, in the sycamore wood on 28 June 1991. It is another typical Celtic depiction, also with a long stretched face, This comprises a deep, wide mouth and ipso-phallic eyes and nose. The eyes are offset.

It is a flat face worked into relief by cutting the soft, gritty non-island Doulting limestone into a triangle with a rounded top. There is a sunken surround at the sides and top of the head. Indentations around the apex represent limed hair which was swept back.

The face has a patina of green algae but the remainder of the stone has been in the ground and is cream with pinkish staining. The size is 8.5 cm wide at the base, with sides of 7.5 cm, and a tapering length of 13 cm.

The long part of the stone is also rounded into a triangle as if to set in a wall. Such stones, of this size, tended to be erected in twos, representing male (this one) and female, in the top left and right corners of Romano-Celtic doorways. This architectural nature of the stone dates it to the late first century AD, or the second century AD, rather than the Iron Age.

These stone carvings are representative of the art-form that was far more widely distributed as wooden totem poles when Saint Gilda was writing his *De Excidio Britanniae* in about 545: "I shall not enumerate those diabolical idols of my country, which almost surpassed in number those of Egypt, and of which we still see some mouldering away within and without the deserted temples, with stiff and deformed features as was customary."

Two carvings, one of them architectural, found around the same spot on an offshore rock, are strong evidence for the existence of a Celtic shrine here in the Severn sea. If a reason for religion is needed, then the treacherous waters would have provided it, and also voyagers as the clientele – making their visits whilst their vessels lay at anchor to await the tide.

Dr Miranda Aldhouse-Green of the School of History and Archaeology at the University of Wales shares my thoughts about the "second" (Harrison Matthews) and "first" (Terry Gore) heads: "Thank you very much for sending me the information on the second Steep Holm head. It really does look genuine, and it is very exciting to have two of them! I quite agree with you about the first head; there does seem to be strong evidence of a sacred building here. Given the fondness of the Celts for islands as sacred places, the idea of a sanctuary seems very promising."

Hilltop and coastal sites were favoured by several cults. Indeed there is a Romano-Celtic temple midway along the spine of Brean Down. I am tempted to imagine that a similar temple pre-dates the Steep Holm Christians and stood a few yards north of the Priory. Bits and pieces of Roman building materials continue to be found in the vicinity, though there is even stronger evidence for a different Romano-British structure at the other end of the island.

Big head: Terry Gore's Romano-Celtic head of architectural-type stone with the end carved in deep relief. Retouched to emphasise the strength of the design – it may well have been painted originally. Photographed, with a £1 coin for scale, by Rodney Legg in 1991.

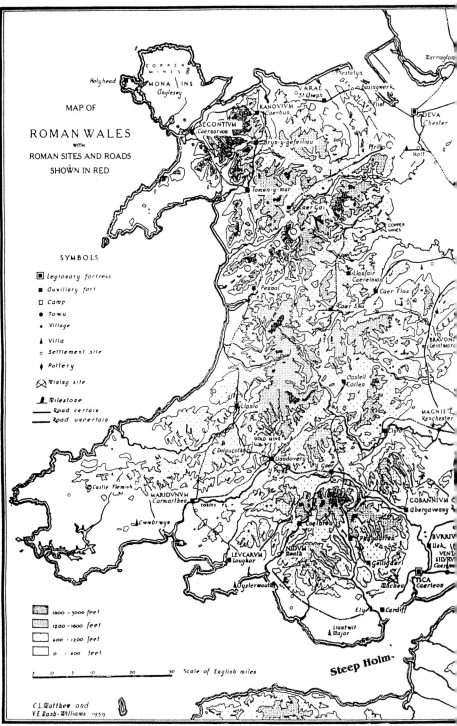

Eyes of the Fleet: Steep Holm (bottom right) was the principal signal station for naval units based at Cardiff, when the Irish plundered Roman Wales. Drawn by C.L. Matthew and V.E. Nash-Williams in 1939.

Roman signal station

It is only since the Kenneth Allsop Memorial Trust bought Steep Holm, and allowed Banwell Archaeological Society to resume the excavation of the Priory site at the east end of the island, that Roman finds have been reported in some quantity. For various reasons, including the type of finds, the strategic position of the island and the existence of a pre-Victorian mound at Rudder Rock, it is presumed that the island was occupied by the Roman military and used as a signal station. Such stations were in use in the Bristol Channel during two principal periods of the four centuries of Roman rule – near the beginning and towards the end.

The first to suggest that there was a signal station on the island was Rev John Skinner of Camerton, near Bath, who visited Steep Holm on 26-27 July 1832, but his description confused me because he thought the dorsal of the island was running north to south rather than west to east. He accompanied his account with a drawing that shows Flat Holm and Penarth Point in the distance and an oval mound in the foreground. It is captioned "Site of a signal beacon or tumulus, but more probably of the former, at the northern extremity of the island facing the coast of Wales". A second, nearer view shows the mound surrounded by a kerb of stones and has the caption: "View of the signal beacon on a larger scale – being about 18 or 20 paces in diameter. It might have been the base of a tumulus as there are several of this diameter but I should think it was a Beacon Barrow."

Stan Rendell pointed out to me that Skinner's text makes it clear that he thought that the "natural doorway" was "Rudder Rock at the northern extremity" and that beyond it was "the Danish Signal post with the path leading to it". Its site has to be the more compacted stones that are still visibly different and form a gentle slope on the lower, western, side of the Victorian mound that covers the underground shell and cartridge stores behind Rudder Rock Battery.

Skinner says "it measures within the oval about 20 paces by 18; the walls formed of loose stones might have been about four feet wide, the uprights being fixed in the soil, or rather the rock, and the inner space filled up very similar to the workmanship of the vitrified forts in Scotland". He calls it "a Danish work" because he had "seen similar remains attributed to this people". The old antiquaries had wrongly assumed that earthworks

45

could be dated simply from their shapes, and declared oval structures to be Danish and square ones Roman.

Interestingly, Skinner also notes "fragments of the grey Roman pottery"and "tiles and bricks" with "some of the former hollowed out after the Roman manner". Skinner was familiar with Roman remains in his own parish and at nearby Bath so by this he is referring to hypocaust flue-tile – at least one confirmed piece of which has been found in the 1977-92 excavations at the Priory. Grey pieces of Roman pottery usually turn out to be black-burnished ware and one particularly gritty example, probably from the kilns beside Poole Harbour, is the side of a collander. It was picked up from amongst the debris brought down into the Inn when the Royal Engineers blasted the cliffside in July 1941.

In my book *Romans in Britain*, published in 1983, I outlined the current state of knowledge of the highly important chain of Roman signal-posts and associated forts that were set-up in the West Country about seven years after the Claudian invasion of Kent that took place in 43 AD. The network seems to have been operational from 50 to 80 AD. It was Graham Webster who had suggested, in the first volume of the journal *Britannia* (the name of the Roman province of Britain), in 1970, that "one might expect more stations of this kind to keep the whole of the Bristol Channel under observation". In 1980 Stan and Joan Rendell pointed out that we might well have one on the island and I summarised the Steep Holm possibilites for my book:

"One strong contender is Steep Holm, a 250-foot high limestone island midway between the Mendip Hills and Wales. There is a mound of stones at its western point, above Rudder Rock, which was incorporated into a Victorian gun battery in 1866. It, and other spots on the island, have yielded first century artefacts."

These include some brooches and other items including a bracelet but the major find, from the side of the great stone-heap at Rudder Rock, was the neck of a Dressel-category Spanish amphora – a large pottery container for the import of olive oil or wine – dated to between 90 and 140 AD. An indicator of Roman occupation at the earliest period, during the first decade of Rome's rule when its forces were still using supplies that had been brought across from the continent, was a sherd found at the other end of the island, a piece of up-market Arretine ware with applied decoration. This was the forerunner of the smooth plastic-looking Samian pottery that has also turned up on the island.

Of the hundred or more Roman potsherds that have been found on the island in the years 1977-92 about ten percent are deluxe Samian or other fine-wares that would not normally comprise the kitchen utensils of the fisher-folk one might expect to find on a fifty-acre rock.

Some of these pieces are early, being fragments of pre-invasion Arretine ware from Italy that would have come across the Channel – the English one – with the Claudian fleet in 43 AD. Most, however, are later Samian copies; the *terra sigillata* of older books on archaeology. The finest piece of the latter, discovered a short distance up from Cliff Cottage when one of Chris Maslen's working parties recut the central incline of the zig-zag path – breaking the said find – amounts to half a Dragendorff type-36 dish with barbotine leaf decoration around its broad, curved rim. The full diameter was 16 cm and it was produced at La Graufesenque, Gaul, probably in the Flavian period of 69-96 AD.

Mortimer Wheeler, in the 1930s, found direct evidence of the sort of units that were on patrol in these waters in the latter part of the fourth century. The *scafae exploratoria*, fast-moving scout craft with camouflaged sails, were the mainstay of the British inshore fleet and its answer to the incursion of Irish raiders who would otherwise have plundered the rich villa-lands of the Welsh and Somerset shores. As Stanley Baldwin said of the bomber, some would slip through, but apart from savage localised incidents the threat of a general disaster was averted. Wheeler discovered one of the navy's places of worship, the Temple of Nodons, at Lydney Park, and in particular a mosaic, dated to after 367, that carried initials thought to be those of the *Praefectus Reliquationis Classis* – the supplies officer of the western fleet. It had a nautical surround of fish and dolphins.

Effective use of Roman seapower depended upon sightings and signals from semaphore stations. These had massive posts set into a mound, rising in a gallows-like construction into great shutters that could be seen for several miles. Cardiff Castle was the main port and garrison of the fleet. Roger J.A. Wilson writes in *Roman Remains in Britain*: "Cardiff cannot have stood alone and must have been linked with a series of signal posts to give warning of imminent pirate raids."

The western end of the island has perfect line-of-sight vision to the entrance of Cardiff harbour. Inside the walls of the island's mediaeval St Michael's Priory, the Rendells have discovered a mass of displaced Roman material including some coins of Constantine that indicated this occupation of Steep

Holm had not just been in the first century but had resumed in the fourth century.

Once again the evidence was not of the fishing-family sort. It included tiling and even a hypocaust wall-flue tile that indicated a building much less basic than one would expect on Steep Holm – a luxury that would require a state-subsidised supply boat to keep in fuel. Later Stanley and Joan would find a piece of engraved green glass from what would have been a magnificent and expensive Hunt-type bowl. That would have been far too precious to have gone to sea with the salad for a Roman picnic party.

In the earlier book I summarised the island's locational case for being the primary offshore signal station to Cardiff castle:

"The finest viewpoint in these waters is the rocky island of Steep Holm, six miles off each coast and midway between Cardiff and the port the Romans used for the lead mines. There is no other point in the Bristol Channel with a panorama that stretches the full seventy miles along the coast of Devon at Ilfracombe along the entire seaboard east to the Severn Bridge, at that time a ferry crossing. Its coverage of the English coastline of the Bristol Channel is unlimited, and on the Welsh side, the view runs from Barry to the Black Mountains. Even small boats can be pinpointed at a considerable distance and their speed and direction accurately gauged. Gun emplacements litter the island cliffs and show its strategic value, which was recognised both in Victorian times and during the Second World War. Steep Holm had the additional attraction for the Romans in that it has a clear view to the mouth of Cardiff harbour, the approaches to their main base."

The other contender for the supply base of Classis Britannica, the Roman fleet, in the Bristol Channel, is an extensive fourth century store that was uncovered in 1980 after demolition work in Barry. It lies behind Bindles Night Club, at the Knap, and has extensive views along the Bristol Channel, across to the Rudder Rock end of Steep Holm. The director of Glamorgan-Gwent Archaeological Trust, Gareth Dowdell, was quoted in The Times of 23 July 1980. He said that when the excavation started he thought he had discovered a Roman villa but that he had become convinced that it was a supply base for the Roman fleet. He believed that the Roman naval defence base at Barry – "Watching for attacks from the Irish" – could rank in importance with Roman sites on the Rhine and at Engers in Germany.

Here I have implied that the Steep Holm signal station would have been crucial in the first and fourth centuries but the story is probably much more complicated. The coin evidence shows that the island has a connection with the troubled times in the late third century when a powerful senator, Gaius Pius Esuvius Tetricus, seized power in Britain, Gaul and northern Spain and declared himself emperor in 270 after the death of Marcus Aurelius Claudius. The usurper Tetricus used the English Channel as his last ditch against Rome but was defeated by an accomplished common soldier, Lucius Domitius Aurelianus, in 274. Meanwhile, in the general period of continental unrest since 260, wealthy refugees from Gallia Belgica had been arriving in Britain and were establishing many of the most prosperous of the villas in south-western England.

The tussle between Roman and Romano-British fleets and armies may explain how a bronze coin of Tetricus came to be found in the excavations of the Steep Holm Priory in 1984. Tetricus had every need for a coast watch, with an influx of craft bringing harmless refugees but the fear for four years that the distant specks might turn out to be the Roman fleet, and it is highly probable that the usurper's men were on the island officially.

The smooth red Samian sherds from Steep Holm that have been found at the Priory and elsewhere in the eastern part of the island have tended to be remarkably clean and unscratched. This indicates that they were breakages which occurred whilst they were still new; the amount of such damaged crockery was probably abnormally high as a result of the island's rough terrain. One piece, however, was abraded from years of use and a scatter of various types of third and fourth century Roman pottery on the central plateau also seems to have been well-used. That said, an abnormally high proportion of these dishes and bowls had only a short shelf and table-life.

Military man, like modern man, is a wasteful species.

Coins of Tetricus: 'barbarous radiates', as they are known to collectors, being British and Continental copies of the usurper's coinage. That his coins arrived on Steep Holm points to landings in those volatile times, when the Romano-British army and fleet clashed with forces from Rome. Photographed by P. Frank Purvey for Seaby's.

Saint Gildas

Longstanding tradition associates the British monk and historian Gildas [?516-570] with Steep Holm. The author of *De Excidio Britanniae*, which charts and laments the decline of Roman Britain into the anarchical Dark Ages, he is known as "Saint Gildas the Wise". John Leland [?1506-52] was King Henry VIII's antiquary, appointed in 1533, who toured Britain searching out records and manuscripts. It was in one of these documents, since destroyed, that he came across references to Gildas and Cattwg Ddoeth [died about 570] who as "Saint Cadoc the Wise" not only shared the Gildas surname but befriended him and taught in his school. Cadoc was the first abbot of Llancarvan Abbey which he had founded in Glamorgan; a successor Caradog [died about 1147] would provide the information that Gildas was buried at Glastonbury. Gildas and Cadoc are credited with tutoring the Welsh bard Taliesin.

Alternative claims for the Gildas burial place were made for Brittany but Leland's information supports the contention that he had returned to Britain. Monasteries on both sides of the water had strong fiscal motives for sustaining the belief that they preserved relics such as his remains. These attracted pilgrims – the tourists of the mediaeval packaged holiday business who were the lifeblood of the grander and more remote religious houses. Even a minor priory, such as that established on Steep Holm in the twelfth century, would have cherished, if not actually invented, a notion that such a famous personage as "Saint Gildas the Wise" had graced their domain.

Leland writes that the saints Gildas and Cadoc (or Cadocus) retired to two islands between the English and Welsh coasts. Cadoc went to the one near Wales, and Gildas to that near England. The islands were not named in the original document but Leland gives them as Ronnet (or Romuth) and Echin (or Echni) which can be translated as Steep Holm and Flat Holm respectively. There can be no doubt about the identity of the two islands as only the Holms have a dual relationship with the English and Welsh coasts.

The name Ronnet or Romuth has to be the one for Steep Holm. The Celtic prefix *ro*, the Welsh *rhy*, implies it is "great" and "large" which perfectly describes the way Steep Holm rears up from the water. This identification is confirmed by William Camden [1551-1623] in his *Britannia*. Steep Holm is mentioned among "The smaller Islands in the British Ocean" in column

1049 of the expanded edition published by Edmund Gibson in 1695. This is the extract, with the long 's' spellings modernised for clarity:

"In the Severn, there first appear two small Islands; the one being plain and level is called *Flatholme*, in the same sense with *Planarie* in Italy; the other being steep, is called *Stepholme*, and in British *Reoric*; but the Britains termed them both *Echni*, as we do now *Holmes*; for so the Saxons always called a grassy plot of ground enclosed with water. Formerly they were famous for nothing else but for the Danes that harbored there; and for the burial of *Gualch*, a Britain of great piety, whose Disciple *Barruch* has given name to the Island Barry in Wales . . ."

There is a further strand to the Gildas connection as set out by John Leland. He read that it was on Steep Holm that Gildas wrote his history of Britain, *Liber Querulus De Excidio Britanniae* (literally, "The book of complaint concerning the downfall of Britain"). Unfortunately, Leland does not give the source of his information, and it has been doubted by subsequent historians. The *Dictionary of National Biography* states that Gildas began writing in Brittany in 559.

Certainly, the character of Steep Holm would have suited the personality and philosophy of Gildas. A spell on an island as a hermit was a common monastic practice in the Dark Ages. Loneliness would probably have suited him as he regarded most other humans as unrighteous. John Fowles, who had reviewed a book on the mental disorder known as "lighthouse-keeper madness" – which occurs when men are put alone on islands – pointed out that such a syndrome might explain the content of his writings. Unfortunately, to quote John Fowles, "it is outrageously unlikely" that these could have been produced on the island. Writing was a complicated business in the sixth century and only a well-equipped abbey like Glastonbury would have been suited for it, with the necessary parchments, ink and pens. Our discussion on the inherent unsuitability of islands as places for writing took place on Steep Holm in 1977 and was scratched on to an ex-Fowles Gauloise packet with a Japanese Pentel that had lost its ball-point.

On the other hand it is reasonable to suggest a connection between Steep Holm and the earliest Glastonbury monks. Steep Holm is clearly visible from Glastonbury Tor, twenty-two miles away, and is marked on the National Trust's bronze plate which identifies the panorama (though with lines that are set about five degrees to the left of the landmarks concerned). Steep Holm must have been the obvious choice for a place of solitude, for monks to show how holy they were, and for Gildas this could have taken place around 540. That would have coincided with the monastic apprenticeship of Cadoc. It is probable that Gildas, who was then in his twenties, stayed on Steep Holm and thought out his philosophy there, even though he could not possibly have written a manuscript on the island.

Then at the age of about thirty-three, in 549, Gildas left Britain – probably from St Illtyd's monastery – for Brittany. He would spend the rest of his life at Ruys, near Vannes, if one discounts the story that he returned to Glastonbury to die. Associations with a famous saint were not only the mainstay of the traffic in pilgrims but were coveted by monasteries for their practical value in encouraging endowments. Such pious lies were commonplace in the early Middle Ages.

Gildas came from a strongly eremitical tradition stemming from St Illtyd and his school in Glamorgan, which evidently had strong Breton links. He is recorded as having spent a time on an island in Brittany called Horata, which makes it a little more likely that earlier in his life he had lived on an island off England. Gildas began writing in his mid-forties, in about 460. He was Roman by culture and politics, at a time when the Saxon onslaughts threatened post-Roman Christian society, and for all the latter-day descriptions of his writings as the "tiresome wailings of a misery" he is the major contemporary source for the history of the early sixth century. He would be remembered at Glastonbury, where 29 January was set aside as the Festival of St Gildas Badonicus (he was born in the year of Arthur's victory at Mount Badon). Gildas was given other nicknames including the "Confessor", the "Albanian", and the confusing "Elder" and 'Younger" (which came about as it was wrongly thought there were two Gildases).

Known more generally as "Saint Gildas the Wise" he is still said to be on the island of Steep Holm in spirit. This manifests itself as a supernatural phenomenon allegedly in the form of the nightly tread of ghostly feet. The tale has persisted from Victorian times to the present – at least if one believes the comments column of the island visitors' book.

Mary Collier from Musbury, near Axminster, was working with me on a collection of the *Ghosts of Dorset, Devon and Somerset* in 1972, before I even knew of the existence of Steep Holm. She found a nineteenth century record of the haunting and gave a short account of the Somerset stage in Gildas's life:

"But although the religious house at Glastonbury was once his home, his ghost haunts Steep Holme. Maybe he loved the little island. He is not seen, but on moonlight nights he is heard nearby the ruin of the Priory, just the slow footsteps of somebody walking along, which are called 'St Gilda's Tread'."

Late twentieth century manifestations of St Gildas's Tread have been heard by people sleeping in the island's Barracks block and described as a "crunching of gravel along the path". This path is now of compacted earth, either side of a wide expanse of flat concrete, and the reports of the treading sounds pre-date the introduction of the island's Muntjac deer in 1977.

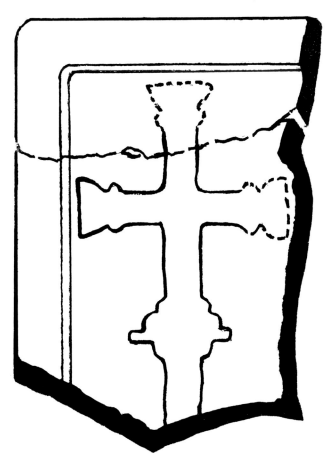

Not for Gildas: the cross of Lorraine on a memorial stone to a Steep Holm Prior of the thirteenth century, discovered in 1867 in the construction of Tombstone Battery and providing its name. Described on page 63. Shown above with dotted lines for lost areas of design, and a fracture across the top, drawn by Rodney Legg in 1992.

The Vikings

Viking raiders took refuge on Steep Holm in the summer of 914, according to three of the four manuscripts of the *Anglo-Saxon Chronicle* that survive. The other version opts for Flat Holm instead, though the balance of probability favours Steep Holm, or indeed both of the islands.

The background to the incursion up the Bristol Channel was that King Edward's Saxon army was locked in an uneasy confrontation with the Danes along an Essex front-line only forty miles from London. In an attempt to outflank the Saxons, in the spring of 914, the Scandinavians mounted a naval attack against Wales and the West Country. Steep Holm came into the picture after the fortunes of the western Viking invaders had been reversed by a land battle near Hereford. Two earls, Ohter and Hroald, were their leaders. The latter was killed and Ohter lost his brother in the action. A truce was called and the Norsemen "gave hostages (promising) that they would leave the king's domain".

The Danes fell back to the Severn seaboard and looked for an offshore refuge. They chose Steep Holm, though it is probable the island had already been utilised, or at least reconnoitred and earmarked at an early stage as the safest point to which to withdraw and regroup in the event of a failure on the mainland. As Paul Chaillu wrote in his 1889 study, *The Viking Age*, the tactics of the Norse fleets "showed considerable boldness and strategical skill, which generally left them with a way of retreat, if necessary, to their vessels or to some island".

This Danish fleet, when it arrived in the Bristol Channel, was described as a "great naval force" but the number of ships is not recorded. The total was certainly substantial and would have been in three figures. In a similar attack on eastern England, in 851, three hundred and fifty Viking longships sailed into the Thames.

From Steep Holm the remnants of the enemy fleet raided the Somerset coast at Watchet and Porlock. In both cases they were repulsed by the Saxon defenders, who were on full alert along the entire coast from Cornwall to Avonmouth, and the longships returned to Steep Holm. Three copies of the *Anglo-Saxon Chronicle* record the basic facts and identify Steep Holm by its old English name, "Steepholme" meaning "Steep grassy island", rather than the Celtic Welsh alternatives of Ronnet, Romuth or Reoric:

"And they remained out on the island of Steepholme until they became very short of food and many men had died of hunger because they could not obtain any food. Then they went from there to Dyfed, and from there to Ireland; and this was in the autumn."

The involvement of Steep Holm in this episode would be completely clear but for the version of the Chronicle at Corpus Christi College, Cambridge, which names "Flatholme" as the island the Danes occupied. The other three copies agree on "Steepholme"; two of them are in the British Museum and the other is in the Bodleian Library at Oxford.

Apart from the odds of three to one in favour of Steep Holm there is supporting negative evidence in that the island's water supply is not mentioned. All four copies of the Chronicle say the Scandinavians left the island because of hunger – which implies that at least the water supply had been adequate. Fresh-water trickles down the north-west cliff of Steep Holm, even today, but there is no natural water available on Flat Holm. That fact, discovered on the reconnoitre, would have made the use of Steep Holm an imperative, though it is also likely that because of its easier beach they would have chosen Flat Holm for any repairs. Frank Watts, with half a century's experience of both beaches, is in no doubt that a landing on Flat Holm would present less problems than at Steep Holm where the only beach projects into a fast flowing tide-race.

An accident seems to have happened to the supplies that should have fed the Severn invaders. Danish forces of this size did not merely comprise troopships but had full naval support including special vessels, the "vista byrding", that carried pro-visions. There is no archaeological evidence to throw any light on the expedition. The Chronicle mentions a prison compound, near Hereford, but it has not been found. neither have battle sites, graves, discarded weapons or any other object.

Somewhere in the Bristol Channel silt there must be Viking swords, or at least their more durable gilded bronze scabbard fittings, and there are probably the remains of some longships under the murky waters. On Steep Holm, even if Viking activity concentrated on the eastern beach, a look-out would have been kept from the site of the Roman signal station at Rudder Rock and there may have been the walls of a Roman ruin to give shelter from the wind. Somewhere there must be traces that answer that nebulous description "artefacts".

Fleeing Saxons

Steep Holm, in many Somerset histories, is credited with being a refuge for fleeing Saxons in 1067. Certainly, the women of England's deposed leadership are known to have stayed on an island in the Bristol Channel, sometime after the Battle of Hastings, while arrangements were being made for their exile in Wales. The island, however, that was used for this refugee camp was not Steep Holm but Flat Holm, and the year is more likely to have been 1068.

The error resulted from past misreading of a passage in the *Anglo-Saxon Chronicle* which when correctly transcribed, in this case by Dorothy Whitelock, reads: "Gytha, Harold's mother, and many distinguished men's wives with her went out to Flatholme and stayed there for some time and so went from there overseas to St Omer."

Shepholme
Island

Mediaeval pirates

Piracy must have had a place in the island's history. As I have pointed out, in considering its almost certain use by the Romans against their Irish problem, no other single point in the Severn seaboard has such an uninterrupted vantage of the entire English and Welsh coasts from the open sea to the inner estuary. It must have been known to William de Marisco, who fled to these waters after being accused of the murder of a London clerk, Henry Clement, in 1235. He was also said to have instigated an assassination attempt on King Henry III, at Woodstock in 1238, and took refuge on Lundy Island where he attracted a number of other desperate outlaws.

By the end of the 1230s they were running a highly efficient piracy operation, which was causing national concern as this is the sea-lane into what was then England's second largest city, the port of Bristol. The Lundy pirates selected incoming ships that were laden with wine and food.

William de Marisco was watched for many months and in 1242 the trap was sprung and he found himself being captured at sea. He was taken to London where he denied the two original charges, though not that of being the most "mischievous pirate" of the age, and was with sixteen of his colleagues taken to the gallows to be disembowelled, then hanged, and quartered.

If nothing else, it would have been the major news event of the year for a tiny community of monks, who were then living on Steep Holm.

OPPOSITE. **Buccaneers: the name is associated with the West Indies and the period of John Speed's county map of Somerset, rather than the earlier pirates of home-waters. The illustration does, however, add a near-contemporary touch, re-drawn by Rodney Legg from mapping detail of 1610.**

'A far-away island of which we know nothing': it is appropriate to paraphrase Neville Chamberlain's words for this is the year of Munich, when Bristol Naturalists' Society mounted an expedition to uncover something of the remains of St Michael's Priory, Steep Holm. Victorian fortifications of Garden Battery are in the background — soon Europe would be at war and these would be demolished and refortified. Seen from the north. Photographed by Leo Harrison Matthews in 1938.

Post-war: a deeper look at the Priory in the 1980s would reveal something of the thirteenth century occupants, this monk being buried beside the north wall. Photographed by Colin Graham in 1984.

Augustinian monks

Until any Roman foundations are discovered on Steep Holm the earliest dateable masonry will be that at the eastern end of the island, at the top of the cliff path, where a flat platform looks out across the sea to Sand Bay, Worlebury, Weston Bay and Uphill. The footings are of a substantial building, its alignment being from east to west, with walls a metre thick. These still stand to a maximum height of 1.5 metres at the west end and are clearly mediaeval in construction, having their typical mix of small stones interspersed with roughly tooled polygonal boulders. Smaller squared stones were used for the door and window openings and there is a moulded base-stone on the only remaining sill. I have found fragments of easily-cut creamy Doulting limestone – which has been previously misidentified as a sandstone – from carved window mullions. These had found their way into the later ruins to the east; the best piece was in the wall of the privy.

Similar but larger, unmoulded, blocks of stone underlie the southern wall of the building at points where its outer side is exposed. It seems such a waste of effort to import stone for foundations when the whole island is solid rock. I therefore wonder whether the mediaeval builders cleared up a Roman ruin and incorporated its larger debris in their own footings.

As the Banwell Archaeological Society uncovered these walls in the early 1980s the building expanded to an impressive size – a rectangle 21.7 metres long by at least 5 metres wide with some internal walls at the west end. Adjoining it, beneath a Second World War Nissen hut, there was apparently an ancillary building at the eastern end of the north side. Along the western end of this side, extending northwards beside the east wall of the 1776-built Tenement, was a graveyard.

The excavation has determined not only the size of the building but also its general appearance. The roof was brown, being covered with slates of Pennant sandstone from Clevedon, with a rippling pie-crust effect to the apex being provided by the attractive green-glazed pottery ridge tiles. Pennant slates are about a foot long and rectangular in shape, with a nail hole near the top, and the bottom corners tapering. There is an exhibit in the archaeological display in the island's Barracks which shows how the slates and their ridge tiles would have been used.

That, briefly, is a description of the building. Nothing has yet been discovered during the excavations which proves its purpose, excepting the discovery of neatly placed graves, with their skeletons beneath *in situ*, against the north wall on the north side. They indicate it was a church.

There is, fortunately, documentary evidence to confirm this. Various rights and lands at Uphill, including the church there, its tithes, and the use of Uphill mill, were granted in the 1190s to the "Church of Saint Michael of Steep Holm". It also owned property at Christon, the placename itself being already religiously loaded, which is a village near Axbridge. It was then known as Churcheston, or variations of that.

Saint Michael was the most popular choice for high ground dedications because he was in Jewish tradition the archangel who captained the armies of heaven. Two other islands, famous "Mounts" on opposite sides of the English Channel, carry his name. The association between St Michael and places that point a finger towards the sky was reinforced by the Cornish legend that the saint had appeared on St Michael's Mount, either in 495 or 710.

As the leader of the angels, St Michael was reputedly the guardian of the Roman Catholic church, which was the state religion at the time of the church on Steep Holm. They would have celebrated the feast of "St Michael and All Angels" on 29 September. The festival of Michaelmas, said to have been instituted in 487, was accompanied in the Middle Ages by the eating of goose. This custom has been erroneously attributed to the fact that Queen Elizabeth happened to be eating the bird at Sir Neville Umfreyville's house on 29 September 1588 when she heard that the Spanish Armada had been defeated.

They were eating the bird because it was Michaelmas, and records show that it was the traditional dish of the day at the time when the Steep Holm community celebrated the name-day of their patron saint. The custom has survived in parts of Catholic Europe. One of the rewards of mediaeval archaeology is that it can be bolstered by a vast accumulation of written records that allow us to have an accurate and colourful picture of daily lives. In this particular instance we can be sure that the monks of Steep Holm kept geese and that they were consuming at least one of them on 29 September.

Another sure fact is that the monks wore black habits. They were popularly, and indeed in some documents, called the "Black Canons". This term is synonymous with mentions of the Augustinian order which provided the monks for Steep Holm. Their other alternative name was the "Austin Friars".

They had appeared in England soon after the Norman conquest and ascribed their origin to St Augustine, the Bishop of Hippo (not to be confused with the St Augustine who converted England to Christianity). Their Aurelius Augustinus [354-430] is famous for the enormous influence of his writings, particularly *De Civitate Dei*, and his autobiography, *Confessiones*. The rules of his monks would require poverty, humility and chastity. Theologically they upheld the doctrine of the free grace and were the rivals of the Dominicans.

Their great moment of pride – if they allowed such human feelings to surface – coincided with their period on Steep Holm. It was in 1256 when the hierarchy of the Church of Rome gave full recognition to their existence with the granting of the constitution of the order by Pope Alexander IV.

Monasticism lapsed on Steep Holm long before Henry VIII's suppression of the religious houses – the Augustinians then had thirty-two – which took place in 1536. All the members of the little Steep Holm community were long dead when the order suffered its greatest humiliation, in 1580, from the best known member it would ever have. Martin Luther was an Augustinian monk.

As for the monks of Steep Holm only three can be named. There is also a paucity of information concerning the establishment of the community. At the time of the Domesday Book, in 1086, the national land survey shows Brean and Burnham (which included Steep Holm) in the possession of Walter de Dowai. By 1100 the tenant was Harold de Ewais. It would be a member of the de Ewais family who would establish the Priory of St Michael on the island, sometime before 1166.

There were two Roberts, father and son, who would head the family. The first enabled the creation of the Priory and the second, at the end of the century, handed over the right of appointing Burnham's parish priest to the Abbot of Gloucester. It might seem logical if Steep Holm Priory had begun as a cell of the Augustinian canons of Woodspring Abbey – just visible from the island on the hillside at the north end of Sand Bay – but our Priory pre-dates the founding of Woodspring. The known documents were transcribed in 1916 by E.H. Bates Harbin for the Proceedings of the Somerset Archaeological and Natural History Society, in a paper entitled "The Priory of St Michael on the Steep Holme".

These mentions, in date order, were as follows:

Reign of Richard I [1189-99] – grant from Robert, son of Richard, to the brethren of "elemosinam Sancto Michaeli de Stepholm" of "Ecclesiam Sancti Nicholai de Uppilla" [the church of St Nicholas at Uphill].

Reign of John [1199-1216] – confirmation by John de Ken of the above grant by Robert, son of Richard, of the Uphill property and rights to the Steep Holm community "Sancte Michaeli de insula que dicitur Stepholm et fratribus" [brethren of St Michael of the island called Stepholm].

Reign of John – confirmation by William, son of Robert de Langator who was the son of Martin, of the grant by Robert de Sancta Cruce, son of Richard de Bichefauda, knight, of a virgate of land [quarter of an acre] at Huppilla [Uphill] to the island church of St Michael.

Early in reign of Henry III [1216-72] – grant from Thomas de Muncketon to the brethren serving God "et ecclesie Beatri Michaelis in Steepeholm" [and the Blessed Michael at Steep Holm], of himself and his lands at Curcheston [Christon], the gift of Robert, son of Richard, which was confirmed to him by John de Ken and Agacia, his wife, the daughter and heir of the said Robert.

October 1236 – hearing before the Michaelmas Assize at Ilchester to confirm the renouncement of the inheritance of half a virgate of land [eighth of an acre] at Kercheston [Christon] in favour of "the Prior and church of Stepholm". Henry, the son of Richard, made the gift to prior William and in return he and his heirs were promised the benefits and prayers of the church of Steep Holm for ever. William is the only island Prior whose name is known to us.

1243 – two lay canons from Steep Holm, Brothers Gregory and Richard, were accused of larceny before the jury of the Winterstoke Hundred. The court handed them back to their Prior for judgement and, one suspects, corporal punishment. The Augustinians were among the orders that practised heavy flagellation. William M. Cooper lists four categories of punishment in *A History of the Rod*, but that for theft is not specified: "In the regular order of St Augustine there were four degrees of penance. The laymen of this order were summoned to the monastery to receive the discipline when they transgressed the rules. If an individual was obstinate, and refused to undress, he was subjected to imprisonment and a heavier punishment. Lying, swearing, and speaking to women, were visited by a discipline on the naked body. Profanation and drunkenness entailed so severe a flagellation that it was almost beyond endurance. A story is told of a doctor having to appear in a miserable gown, being made to undress to the waist, and run the gauntlet of the scourging brotherhood."

1260 – a more informative document makes it clear that the Priory's patron was Robert de Tregoz, that it was now a cell of Stodleigh [Studley], Warwickshire, and that it was required to have two canons living there – implying that the population had dropped to that of just a hermit. The charter was among a vast collection that were sorted out by I.H. Jeayes of the British Museum in the muniment room of Berkeley Castle, Gloucestershire, between 1886 and 1892. It is the deed of William Bitton, Bishop of Bath and Wells, "ordaining that for the purpose of achieving the most frequent celebration of divine service at the religious place called Stepholm, which island Robert de Tregoz had conferrred on the Austin canons of Stodleigh, the Prior shall cause at least two canons to reside on the island. Of these, the senior canon would be known as the Prior of Stepholme".

Studley Priory was in severe debt and Godfrey Gifford, Bishop of Worcester from 1268 to 1302, wrote an undated begging letter to another Augustinian community in the diocese, asking if they would take care of two brethren for eighteen months. Bates Harbin, who found this letter in the library of Corpus Christi College, Oxford, writes:

"One is tempted to surmise that they may be the couple who ought to have been sojourning on the Steepholme."

1265 – Robert de Tregoz's patronage of Steep Holm ended with his death at the Battle of Evesham. Bates Harbin says "It is now quite evident that Robert de Berkeley was the person who really benefitted by the abandonment of the Priory" but he does not explain why an unihabited island should be regarded as such an asset to the Berkeley family. It would be used by rabbit warreners but even that would be only a marginal luxury to an estate which could have afforded much greater extravagances.

circa 1320 – Maurice, Lord Berkeley [1281-1326] is credited by John Smyth, in his *Lives of the Berkeley Family* which was written in the late 1500s, with having "re-built the friary for the fryers and breathren in the Holmes, an Iland in Seavern, and not far from his manor of Portbury". No records, however, have come from any fourteenth century source to support this statement.

The finest of the remains associated with the Priory is part of a thirteenth century blue lias memorial slab with the top of a Lorraine-type cross with double bars, the sort adopted by the Free French forces in the Second World War, which was found during the 1867 fortification of the island. It was built into the sidearms store of the battery to which it gave a name, Tombstone Battery, on the north side of the Priory and its graveyard.

A Victorian inscription on the stone recorded: "Excavated near this spot 1867."

As the tombstone was built into a wall on the north-west side of the Priory, it is reasonable to suppose the cemetery lay between the Priory buildings and the northern cliffs. This has since been partially confirmed by the finding of a skeleton aligned from east to west beside the north wall of the Priory; in all probability there are many more between the Priory and the remains of the sidearms store. Several arrangements of rectangles of small stones uncovered in 1987-88 look to me like the kerbings and coverings of graves. I predicted this location would yield graves, in *Steep Holm – a case history* in 1978, because the cemetery seemed unlikely to have been on the other side of the Priory, as the ground there, at Garden Battery, is the most sheltered on the island and too useful to be sacrificed for burials.

John Barrett has recorded the moving of the memorial stone to its safer location in the island Barracks: "During Whitsun 1959, members of the Folk House Archaeological Club removed part of the stone coffin lid from the wall of the Tombstone Battery's sidearm store. The piece of lid, which is of a moulded hard blue lias, has a cross cut into the surface. The lid was removed in a broken condition and is now housed in the small museum at the Barracks, where it has been cemented on to a large slate."

It is not, in fact, a coffin lid but an above-ground flat memorial stone, highly polished and intended to be visible. The moulded sides show that it was not made to fit on a stone coffin. Leo Harrison Matthews, who excavated the Priory in 1938, made the same mistake. A considerable quantity of human bones were dug from the Priory ruins in June 1977 by a London schoolboy, the appropriately named Diggory Sladden, in an unauthorised excavation. He found the bones, which would fill two large boxes, "hard against the inside of the south wall of the Priory" about sixteen feet west from its south-east corner. They were from at least nine skeletons, seven being adult males, one a woman, and the other a 14-year-old boy.

Traditionally, bones have repeatedly been found on Steep Holm. Rev John Skinner, when he visited the island on 26 July 1832, was told by an old man that when he dug his garden he uncovered a stone vault seven feet long by four feet wide that contained a human skull and skeleton as well as sheep skulls. "Many human bones have been found in this island," a newspaper reported in October 1885.

Re-excavation of Diggory's hole was carried out on 19 June 1977 by Colin Clements, assisted by Stan and Joan Rendell. "We are now quite positive that the bones Diggory found were a Victorian re-burial," Stan Rendell said. "Beside the hole, in adjacent undisturbed soil, we quickly found further bones lying in situ. These were a complete jumble, and like those already excavated by Diggory, had been damaged and broken at the time of re-burial, before being thrown in a heap." With the bones the excavators found some fragments of a green Victorian beer bottle and a small shard of willow-type pottery. The bones, they considered, where contemporary with the Priory ruin itself and made it abundantly apparent that the builders of the 1867 fortifications had cut their way through the monks' cemetery.

The ruins of the Priory stood "to the height of seven feet, faced with the dressed stone of the island" in 1866-67. Then, with gangs of navvies to be accommodated, even ruined space was at a premium. Given its convenient location at the top of the island, immediately above the landing beach, the Priory was probably the initial dump for building materials and the depôt for the clerk-of-works. Later, its last walls were literally to become part of those war-works, being pulled down and used in the foundation of Garden Battery. Francis Knight, in *The Seaboard of Mendip*, which was published in 1902, mentions both the re-use of the surviving parts of the Priory and the discovery of the bones:

"During the construction of Garden Battery, built on the alleged site of the Prior's garden, the foundations of the Priory were in a great part laid bare. One chamber was in such good repair that it was used as living quarters by the foreman. In clearing out the earth to lay a wooden floor the whole space was found to be packed with skeletons laid close together side by side only a few inches below the surface. Nearby, many bones of deer, brass rings of primitive workmanship, a coin with the figure of an archer, as well as many old pieces of money said to show no legible inscription or device [design] were found. There is a tradition that a former tenant of the island dug up a pot of coins, but of them there is no trace now known."

In the excavations carried out by the Rendells to reach the mediaeval floor-level, or bed-rock, it seemed at times as if the soil was stuffed with the same artefacts. There was a bronze bracelet and the coins with gods and statues were Roman. Some pieces of pottery were contemporary with the Priory, such as a piece of Barnstaple ware and a shard of a polychrome French wine jug, but these were intermingled with the glossy patterns of Victorian kitchen-ware. The whole of the western end of the Priory had been levelled off with wheelbarrow loads of an admixture of Roman, monastic, post-mediaeval and nineteenth century earth and debris.

The dating of the in-fill was confirmed by the find of an 1864 sixpence. It was no longer of more than archaeological curiosity, having ceased to be legal tender in the late 1970s, but I remarked that to its loser it would have been worth the equivalent of five pounds in modern money.

In the second stage of their excavations the Rendells re-dug and levelled the old trenches at the eastern end of the Priory. These had been left to collapse by previous excavators but the site is now grassed and fringed with specimens of the introduced flora that is another legacy of the monastic occupation. Here Leo Harrison Matthews set about digging in 1938 and followed the inside of the east wall to bedrock at a depth of four feet six inches. It is three feet thick and at that time still had traces of plaster. Harrison Matthews noted that the walls of the Priory had been removed to ground level and "not just collapsed inwards". His pottery list, however, is an unsubstantiated jumble of vague type names which is devalued by the inclusion without further comment of "the foot of a Neolithic bowl" – which as I pointed out earlier is very likely to be a case of mistaken identity – though the list should have forewarned the Rendells of the sheer number and variety of potsherds that they were going to be taking home to their garage: "Many pieces of coarse unglazed earthenware which might be assigned to any date during the last thousand years, were found. With them were associated fragments of buff-coloured mediaeval ware with greenish glaze, sixteenth and seventeenth century reeded ware, and shards of modern china. Several pieces of dressed freestone were also found, some with dowel holes; these had evidently formed part of the window of an ecclesiastical building, presumably the Priory."

The bones found by the 1938 excavators included those of sheep, young oxen, pig, and a horse tooth, but some human remains were found in 1962 when Edmund Mason re-opened the north-eastern interior of the Priory. He made the following notes about these bones: "Part of maxillae of adult containing two molars and two premolars (right side). Only portion of palate of roof remaining shows the grooves for the greater palatine nerve vessels. Interior base of maxillary sinus exposed. One adult phalange."

66

Much of the remainder of Mason's material was post-mediaeval and indicated a degree of occupation on Steep Holm in subsequent centuries; in fact the re-use of the building would be proved by the Rendells in the 1980s. Mason was also more adept than Harrison Matthews at the identification of the pottery. L. Hancock, who had excavated the Ham Green kiln, near Bristol, was invited to the island and confirmed that shards were from a jug that had been made at that pottery in about the year 1200.

The most significant structural find of the 1938 dig was "a recent hearth of loosely laid bricks surrounded by much ash" which was thought to show the site of the room fitted out for the Victorian works foreman. Harrison Matthews pointed out: "Certainly the east wall must have been standing to some considerable height in recent time, for such a hearth would be made only within a building of some sort."

To the north of the Priory ruin they found "an area of ground covered with loose stones covering a low mound". They thought this might "represent the disintegrated ruins of a building". The party did not have time to dig into this and it is now covered by scrub. The concrete base of a Nissen hut extends northwards from the eastern side of the north wall of the Priory, but though the outer foundations of this wartime structure will have sliced through the ground, the inner skin of concrete cannot have reached mediaeval levels.

The major disappointment arising from all this disturbance of the eastern end of the Priory, out of necessity in Victorian times and inquisitiveness in this century, is that it has destroyed what traces may otherwise have survived of the stone-built altar that the building would have possessed. Veteran archaeologist C.A. Ralegh Radford visited the island in the early 1980s and showed his penchant for seizing upon echoes of folk memory and giving them new life. "The altar would have been here," he pontificated from the centre of the new lawn the Rendells had planted, as he stood six feet from the middle of the eastern wall. "And what's more, it should be rebuilt!"

Another romantic spot, with something to show both on and below ground, is the Monks' Well. It lies fifty metres north-west of Cliff Cottage, set in a cliff-edge niche beneath a clump of elder bushes, and it is now reached by a flight of concrete steps that were built by Chris Maslen and Jenny Smith in 1986. The armoured steel lid was added by wartime troops in 1941-43, but beneath it is two metres deep and reaches yellow iron-stained rock on a drainage fissure that did not dry in the 1976 or 1984 droughts. The sea, at high tide, is thirteen metres below and the cliff-edge is only a metre and a half from the top of the well. If you look up from the beach below you can see a resurgence of spring water, which is the underground overflow from the well, on the cliff-face about a third of the way down.

The priory also seems to have had its island gatehouse, somewhere on the first shelf up from the beach – on or near the site of the present Inn – which effectively acted as the island's gate. It would have been manned by the Priory's secular attendant who was possibly also their boatman. Monastic houses were strict in keeping the wider world outside their walls and communities often grew up immediately beyond the main gates of their establishments. On Steep Holm there would have been a similar desire to ensure their detachment and privacy.

Beside the gatehouse was the gate. This seems to have been an impressive structure, leaving ruins that were mentioned by later visitors, and in particular a massive arched piece of yellowish Doulting stone. This was a metre long and had been spotted among the beach pebbles in 1986. Though partially eroded it was clearly a huge block of moulded, monastic stone. It was manouevred on to the shelving rocks south of the Inn's sea-door and lashed to an eye-ring there with the intention of a later rescue attempt that would bring it on to the island.

A fortnight later, however, it had gone. The sea had snapped it at the centre of the curve and taken both pieces back into the pebbles.

It is inevitable that there are lapses in our knowlege, both from the records and the archaeology, but there is far more to the story – both generally and then in the specific question of the unique flora of the island and its origin with those thirteenth century monks. This is one of the great surprises that awaits visitors, and the whole plant question deserves detailed examination. I will first outline the general prospects for semi-self-sufficiency upon Steep Holm and then devote a separate section to the complexities of the surviving indicator species that were almost certainly mediaeval introductions to the island.

The existence of a Priory on Steep Holm is significant as part of a wider pattern. The Ordnance Survey's *Map of Monastic Britain* shows the sporadic use of islands for outlying cells of abbeys. In south-west England there were offshore establishments at Tresco in the Scilly Isles, Lammana off Looe, and evidence of a hermitage being established by the monks of Cerne Abbas on Brownsea Island in Poole Harbour, though the latter site, mentioned in my book *Brownsea – Dorset's Fantasy*

Island, is not included on the map.

In the Bristol Channel region, Steep Holm alone has been used for this purpose, and there are no signs that monastic, as distinct from ecclesiastical occupation, took place either on Flat Holm or Lundy. Off the two tips of Wales, monastic houses occur on the islands of Caldy, St Tudwals, Bardsey and Anglesey, together with that isle's two offshoots, Holy Island and Puffin Island. The last site, Puffin Island, used to be called Priestholm and has an affinity with Steep Holm in that it too is overgrown with Alexanders, which was in both cases introduced by monks as a pot-herb.

Such plants provide an explanation of how such tiny communities managed to survive. The lack of an apparent self-sufficiency has puzzled historians. As Bates Harbin notes, the odd half virgates and the rights to graze four cows and twenty sheep at Uphill, and the tithes of that parish, formed only a "very slender endowment" even with the island's sixty acres – that includes ten acres which only appear at low tides, but then that did provide the limpets – being taken into account. They would have had to live off the land and one of the attractions of islands for monks was practical rather than religious. Because of the absence of predators, rocks have teeming seabird colonies. For a limited number of people, and especially a community that was non-breeding, they could provide a dependable food supply that could be made to stretch the year. Puffin, for example, tastes similar to pigeon when fresh, and can be dried in the sun and then stored for winter. T.C. Lethbridge writes that the diet of the Westmann Islands, off Iceland, was puffin for five main meals a week.

Rabbits, conveniently, had been introduced to Britain by the Normans and adapted perfectly to island life. On an island man could be the only predator, without having to compete with the professional work of the foxes, and the rabbit has a breeding rate that can match regular culling. Having a close and easy food supply would have given the monks time for their meditations, and on Steep Holm, herbal horticulture.

That would have taken place on the sunny side of the Priory, and indeed the name of Garden Battery, chosen by the Victorians who fortified the island, perpetuates the tradition that it is on the site of the monks' smallholding. The island's bizarre flora is still dominated by plants that could only have been monkish introductions. The country's medicines were herbal, and the monks were the masters of those arts. They found on Steep Holm a microclimate where a wide variety of tender species would flourish.

To the surprise of many visitors, the eastern top of the island is often wind-free because the thirty degree slope of the surrounding cliffs tends to deflect the air currents upwards, and the Priory is then the most pleasant spot on the island. It is a fact also appreciated by the butterflies. The position of the Priory building itself would have given added protection to the area that is traditionally known as "The Garden" in that it would have blocked the north wind. In a wide variety of conditions it is the stillest and warmest place on the top of the island.

There are cultivation terraces, now almost inaccessible, on the south-facing cliff south-west from the Priory. These lie between the Barracks and the South Landing, on the western side of the remains of a zig-zag path up the cliffs, which is itself to the west of the present cliff path. There is no possibility that these ruined walls were part of a path system as they block the way of anyone trying to climb up between the outcrops. These are difficult and jagged and prevent any movement in the other directions, either to the east or the west, and instead the ruined walls seem to have supported short terraces in a sheltered hollow. To visit them, when a drought makes such an incursion possible by opening up routes into the normally impenetrable vegetation, is to realise the hot-house conditions that they offer.

The island's microclimate has been studied by Clevedon dentist Peter Tailby who established a weather station on the island in 1980. This showed that the average island daytime temperature is five percent warmer than on the mainland and that at night, because of the moderating influence of the sea, which holds down the rate of temperature loss, it rises markedly to ten percent higher than the local mainland figures.

NEXT PAGES, overleaf. **Mass grave: monastic bones in a collective reburial, probably from 1866 when much of the Priory was disturbed in the massive building operations of Victorian fortification. They are seen being drawn by Stanley Rendell with wife Joan head-down in the background as she measures the depth of a find from a levelling pole. Photographed by Colin Graham in 1984.**

Augustinian grave: stones beside the north wall of the Priory, cover the bones of a thirteenth century monk (above left, and below). Seen, above, from the east and below, with Salman Legg, from the north. The third picture, also featuring Salman, shows a pile of architectural debris from the Priory building. Roofing slates of Pennant sandstone in the foreground and moulded window mullions beneath the tabby cat. Photographed by Rodney Legg in 1992.

Light touch: life on Steep Holm has changed little since the demise of monks in the Middle Ages (opposite). The Barracks has lighting of sorts, displayed by volunteer worker Martin Payne (above) tinkering with an aptly named hurricane lamp and Paul Stone (below) relying on candle-power. Photographs by Rodney Legg in 1991-92 and Colin Graham (opposite) with a monastic face none too happy at seeing the light in 1984.

Meadow of Alexanders: the mediaeval pot-herb has escaped its monastic gardeners and smothers Steep Holm. Seen from the south-east, near the Ordnance Survey triangulation pillar (top left) which it has almost engulfed. Photographed by Rodney Legg in 1992.

Spectacular flower: the Wild Peony is the island's floristic treasure, also courtesy the monks. Photographed by Colin Graham in May 1974.

Unique monastic flora

The proof that the monks grew strange, imported plants is all around you on Steep Holm. More than anywhere else in Britain the flora is the living archaeology and the bizarre mixture of species astounds visitors who have been expecting a grassy rock. Add to that the inevitability that other unusual plants will have subsequently become extinct (islands suffer a net loss of species due to the impossibility of normal re-colonisation). Steep Holm has a unique flora because of the survival of seven species that would not normally be found upon a rocky island in north-western Europe. These are the Wild Peony, Wild Leek, Caper Spurge, Alexanders, Henbane, Hemlock and Cuckoo Pint.

Such plants provided the raw materials for the drugs of the Middle Ages and the part abbeys and monasteries played as centres of learning in no way excluded medicine. There is ample historical evidence of the importance of the religious houses as prototype hospitals. For example, Professor H.P.R. Finberg in *Lucerna*, a group of studies of early English history, gives details of a property squabble between Glastonbury Abbey and the Norman owner of Uffculme in Devon. This owner had arrived at Glastonbury in 1086, to argue his case, but fell ill. "He sent three times," to the Prior, "to beg that he might be clothed in the monastic habit: a very common request in such cases, for if granted it secured for the petitioner skilled medical attention in the infirmary."

The author John Fowles spelled out the implications of this: "Glad the Uffculme incident could be fitted in – its real import is of course that powerful abbeys like Glastonbury used their medical expertise to blackmail people they were having trouble with – if you had to take monastic vows to get into the infirmary, you had to renounce your worldly property ... and no guesses needed as to the likely beneficiary."

John Fowles is an accomplished amateur plantsman as well as a knowledgeable theoretical botanist. When as the first chairman of the Kenneth Allsop Memorial Trust he was introduced to Steep Holm in 1974 it was the flora that amazed him. He anticipated the maritime crevice-growing species of the cliffs but was astounded by the appearance of the top of the island which was more like an overgrown garden than a piece of limestone habitat. He wrote to me:

"Although speculation is inevitably involved, the twentieth

century visitors to Steep Holm may be fairly certain that a high proportion of the plants they see were once the raw material of a monastic pharmacopoeia. No doubt most of the medicine was intended for members of the order; but a knowledge of simples in an age powerless against disease was plainly an important advantage, both in worldly and Christian terms. The poor could be helped, the rich made suitably grateful."

To John Fowles it was the flora that answered a question he had posed himself. Why had the monks chosen Steep Holm? He reflected: "So many of the introduced and native plants have important herbal medicine uses that one may plausibly wonder whether the Priory was not regarded more as an extension of the garden of the mother foundation than as a place for solitary contemplation."

Now to the key plants themselves. Firstly and famously there is the Wild Peony *Paeonia mascula* which occurs as a truly wild plant nowhere else in the British Isles; its entry in the Cambridge *Flora* gives no other location. Other places have their clumps of Wild Peony – such as that flourishing across the water on Flat Holm – but only from twentieth century introductions of either its tubers or seed. Other plant books, such as the Collins *Pocket Guide to Wild Flowers*, are also specific on this point: "Long naturalised on Steep Holm in the Bristol Channel." Peonies used to be found wild in Britain in woods near Winchcombe in Gloucestershire, a place with the same type of historical connections, since it was the capital of Mercia and had a monastery in the eighth century.

Sir Frederick Stern, author in 1946 of *A Study of the Genus Paeonia*, believed the Wild Peony was indigenous only to the centre of France, in the departments of Loir et Cher and the Cote d'Or, and to an area near Reichenhall in southern East Germany. Elsewhere, he thought, it had been introduced by monks. It survives as a wild plant in Cyprus, Sicily, Syria, Steep Holm and northern C.I.S. Armenia: "In all these places there may have been monasteries in the past, and it is possible these plants are descended from plants growing in monastery gardens for the medicinal properties credited to peonies in the old herbals."

Mrs M. Grieve, in her famous *Modern Herbal*, says that the powdered root was used to combat convulsions and epilepsy and was especially efficacious against lunacy. John Gerard, in his herbal of 1597, recommends fifteen seeds (which would be three packets if bought from the island's twentieth century shop) in wine or mead against "the disease called the Nightmare". Peony-water was also widely used in mediaeval medicine and the seeds were sometimes crushed as a cooking spice. The last recipe to require their use was published in 1796.

Wild Peony was in classical times regarded as a plant from the moon, with powerful magic properties, which was protective of flocks and harvests. Even in the Mediterranean, as on Steep Holm, its lushness seems out of place in dry and otherwise desolate cliffsides. The tight shoots push phallic-shaped from the ground in the first burst of spring and become a two feet high mass of shiny leaves by late April. These leaves are a light green shade and more rounded, being less divided by indentations, than those of the familiar garden cultivars. It flowers for scarcely seven days, early in May after a mild winter or in the middle or end of that month if conditions in February have been severe, with large scented purplish-pink flowers. The main difference in these between the Wild Peony and cultivated varieties is that the Steep Holm flower-heads comprise five to eight single, instead of multiple, petals. Most of the gardened cultivars do not even derive from the Wild Peony, *Paeonia mascula*, but are instead related to another peony from half-way across the world, the Asian *P. lactiflora*.

A further difference is that the Wild Peonies of Steep Holm set pods that open in October to reveal a striking array of black (fertile) and red (infertile) seeds. These appear when the stems and leaves have completely died back and dried brown on to their stalks. There are some forty to fifty seeds of each colour strikingly visible on the average pod. It is only now that the seed can be taken with any hope of result; yet, each summer, green pods have been removed by those who should know better, that is plant collectors who come to the island with their pen-knives and leave headless stems. Making the seed available legitimately, by selling it with cultivation notes as a souvenir of the island, has lessened the vandalism but such incidents still occur.

These growing instructions of mine may be usefully repeated here, in that they show it is a tricky commodity that requires patience: "Plant in a light position, open to at least half the day's sun. Pots are not recommended because they are likely to dry out during the lengthy germination period, or alternatively to be over-watered, but if you use them make sure they are put outside for exposure to frost during the first and second winters. This frosting is essential to trigger the seeds. Ensure a well drained soil and avoid the use of peat or compost. Any ordinary garden soil, whether it is alkaline or not, will be better than one with chemical or organic additives. Allow two to three years for germination. Appears with a trefoil seedling leaf on a pink stem. Discourage competing vegetation. Keep a dry surface around young plants and avoid mulching as this causes mildew or brown-rot at ground level. They are slow growing and reach only about eight inches in height after four years."

The first recorded discovery of the Wild Peony on Steep Holm was made by F.P. Wright in 1803. One has to admit that other plant collectors had visited Steep Holm, as early as about 1560, and failed to find it. The answer is that they missed the short flowering period and were on the island at a time when it was uninhabited. Even now, despite conservation measures, the Wild Peony is highly localised and the island in the post-monastic period would have been a difficult place to search, before a regular trail of visitors were available to keep open a well-marked perimeter path. Until the sensational discovery of 1803, botanists would not have been expecting to find Wild Peony; by late June and July it would be well camouflaged in the background clutter of ubiquitous Alexanders. The Nature Conservancy verdict is that the plant, in all probability, is a monkish introduction: "There is little doubt that it was introduced, probably by the monks who occupied the thirteenth century Priory. In Europe it is similarly associated with ancient monastic establishments."

The Conservancy also considers the Wild Leek *Allium ampeloprasum* to be a probable ancient introduction to the island. To eat the leek, an expression used by Shakespeare in *Henry V*, was to swallow one's words: "By this leek, I will most horribly revenge." The oldest reference to the Wild Leek on Steep Holm is an item about a "kind of wild Garlicke" in the 1625 account book of the manor of Norton Beauchamp. John Ray [1627-1705] the naturalist knew it was on the island in 1668. He had been told by his friend James Newton [1639-1718], a physician, who also informed James Petiver [1663-1718], another botanist. Ray published first and enumerated the plant in his *Catalogus Plantarum Angliae* Appendix of 1670 with the name *Allium Holmense sphaerico capite*. Professor William T. Stearn confirms in his *European Alliaceae* that this is "the basis of the name *A. holmense* erroneously attributed by many authors to Miller and hence of *A. ampeloprasum* var *holmense Ascherson & Graebner*".

This clarification of the Steep Holm connection is important because the island represents the classic sanctuary for this rare plant. Indeed, Carl von Linné [1707-78], who as Linnaeus created the structure for systematic botany, gives the distribution of the Wild Leek as the Orient and Steep Holm –"Habitat in Oriente, inque insula Holms Angliae". His "parva insula Holms dicto supra Bristolium in Sabrinae aesturario" is Steep Holm island in the Bristol Channel, the Sabrina estuary of the Romans. Stearn emphasises in his interpretation that the specimens in question were not "wild plants but from the old cultivated stock".

Wilde-Duyfjes produced the *Taxon* for the species in 1973 and designated the specimen that is named *Allium holmense sphaerico capite*, in volume 152 of the *Sloane Herbarium*, folio l53 as the lectotype of *A. ampheloprasum L*. "This is a very poor specimen," Stearn writes, "lacking bulb and leaves and the lower part of the scape, and Linnaeus himself never saw it, but the Steep Holm Allium can nevertheless be reasonably accepted as representing the old cultivated stock of northern Europe which Linnaeus had in mind.

"It is illustrated by Sowerby and Smith [1807], Syme [1869] and Butcher [1961]. The island has been uninhabited for many years but the Allium still grows there, having persisted for over three centuries. Examination at the Jodrell Laboratory, Kew, of living plants brought from Steep Holm showed this to be hexaploid ($2n = 48$)."

Stearn's paper on the *European Alliaceae* was published in the Greek scientific periodical *Annales Musei Goulandris* [Volume 4, 1978] and the Steep Holm references are on page 173.

As the president of the Linnaean Society in London, Professor Stearn was concerned about the future of the Wild Leeks on the island, and wrote to me in March 1980 that their presence "makes the island internationally important" and stressed: "The plants of *Allium ampeloprasum* on Steep Holm are the only ones in the world of which we can be reasonably certain that they represent the old cultivated stock of this species unaffected by new introductions during the past three centuries. The importance of this lies in the cytological diversity of *A. ampeloprasum* within the Mediterranean region which is the subject of continuing and revealing research in Israel, Sweden, Spain, Italy and here. Sooner or later cytotypes within this polyploid group will need to be designated. For this the Steep Holm population is crucial because it alone can be taken as the *Allium ampeloprasum* of Linnaeus, sensu stricto, in a living state for cytological purposes.

"I succeeded some years ago after much difficulty, not knowing whom to approach, in getting two bulbs from Steep Holm which proved to have chromosomes $2n = 48$, but more material

81

is needed for investigation of the caryotype. Living bulbs, when they have become dormant, or seed if these are not available, would be welcome later in Jerusalem, Pisa, Seville, Uppsala and Cambridge as representing *Allium ampeloprasum L.* (sensu stricto)."

I was able to reassure him that although, when we first came to the island, the last remaining clump of leeks was sliding into the sea, we had rescued these bulbs. They had been replanted much higher on the eastern ledges and were thriving. In fact the population of Wild Leek has increased during the period 1973-92 from a handful of endangered specimens to what must now be several hundred bulbs. Fortunately, both for them and for me, the plants are ignored by the island's Muntjac deer. Transplanting the bulbs has proved to be the only way of keeping the Wild Leeks growing on the island because although they have impressive flower heads the seed has proved infertile. In the past the plants have gradually fallen down the cliffs, from one rock-fall to the next, and moved from "The Garden" at the Priory to the shore-line below. Until 1974 they occurred only on the extremity of this south-eastern corner of the island and were literally disappearing into the sea. In the absence of fertile seed they had no means of moving back up the cliffs and were becoming victims of erosion and gravity.

Leek is edible, which speaks for itself, but the plant was also endowed with healing properties at least to the extent that it was regarded as a cure-all by an expatriate lady who was writing to me from Switzerland in 1975 and desperately anxious to obtain some bulbs. As that coincided with its nadir, being washed from its last shelf on our splash-zone, she was unlucky.

The third of the island's unusual introductions is barely eatable in any form. That is the Caper Spurge, *Euphorbia lathyrus*, a milk-plant, which grows biennially to three feet in a "highly distinctive, 'architectural' appearance" to use the Collins Guide description. Its leaves are bluish-green, succulent-looking, and arranged in a perfectly ordered series of projecting layers. This plant was the "most used" purgative of John Gerard's famous herbal – its white latex sap the "strong medicine to open the bellie".

That is to put the matter mildly. It is in fact a violent poison and it was only in minute doses that it was administered as a (strong) purgative. The root is equally emetic. The leaf-sap can produce blisters and used to be used by dishonest beggars to increase the sympathy factor.

It is possible, but unlikely, that the Caper Spurge is a native of

English woods. Far more probable is that it was introduced to this country, and certainly to this offshore island, for medicinal purposes. Caper Spurge is a rarity as a wild plant though fairly frequent as a garden weed as a result of the belief in Victorian times that its presence would repel moles.

On Steep Holm it was to have a worthy discoverer. Sir Joseph Banks [1743-1820], the founder of Kew Gardens, visited the island in 1773. Two years earlier he had returned with the first global plant collection, accumulated on Captain Cook's round-the-world voyage in the *Endeavour*. Joseph Banks, as he then was – he would be created a baronet in 1781 – was the first to record the Caper Spurge on Steep Holm. There is no other spot in Britain where it has a recorded history of more than two centuries.

The fourth of the island's historic introductions for us to consider is the one that it is impossible for any visitor to miss. William Turner was the first to metion it in print, in the 1562 *Seconde Parte of W.T.'s Herball*. It is the Alexanders (the confusing "plural" name which applies even to single plants is probably a case of a lost apostrophe and definite article – *id est*, "Alexander's Herb"). Its scientific name, *Smyrnium olusatrum*, derives from its other name by which it was known to the old herbalists, that of "the Black Pot-herb". The black parts of the plant are its seeds, hence the *olusatrum* specific name – *olus* being a pot-herd, and *atrum*, black. Its former Latin name was *Petroselinum alexandrinum* – in old French *alexandre* – from which its common English name derives.

Its stems were blanched, as we do with celery, and it was much eaten at Lent, apparently because it was regarded as having mildly purging qualities. It has an exceedingly strong and lingering taste, which may have been regarded as normal to the mediaeval palate but does not appeal to modern visitors to the island. The flavour reminds me of the old English humbug sweets, for the bitterness but without the saving grace of the sugar, not that they are much more appealing.

Macgregor Skene, in 1939, described the "meadow" of Alexanders on the island plateau as "a society which is certainly unique in this country". It does, however, have monastic Puffin Island as competition though there the colder winters keep it under better control. Naturalised from the Mediterranean, Alexanders grows best in the mild conditions above the sea, and in *The Englishman's Flora*, Geoffrey Grigson provides the clue to its patchy distribution: "In England and Ireland you will find it often by the ruins of castles and abbeys."

The island also has the most powerful sedative in British herbal medicine. "Young plants of Henbane I observed on the top of the island," Somerset botanist Thomas Clark noted in 1831. Henbane, *Hyoscyamus niger*, is a member of the potato family and was familiar in Anglo-Saxon medicine under the name Henbell, from its attractive cream and purple flowers. Its leaves provide the alkaloid hyoscine and juice from the seeds is "very effectual in easing the pains of the teeth". Useful as a hypnotic and anti-spasmodic drug, and as an analgesic, it is highly poisonous, to the extent (visitors be warned) that even the inhalation of vapour from its crushed leaves is dangerous. Curiously its foliage was being pecked down by the island's herring gulls, in their population peak of the 1970s, apparently without harm to them.

Neither did it seem to harm the eight-year-old nephew of a worried vicar. The adult had encouraged the child to eat a young leaf from the base of a flowering plant, knowing that to be Henbane but thinking the lower leaf was "sea cabbage". The misidentification was then pointed out to him but the hairy grey leaf seemed to have no effect upon the lad. Unlike the time when an entire mediaeval monastery once supped on the roots in mistake for those of chicory. All entered a delirious frenzy, had hallucinations, and behaved like lunatics. Its power as an hallucigen made Henbane a favourite constituent of the witches' brew.

Widely distributed across the island, and noted by Joseph Banks in 1773, is the ultimate in potent medicine. Hemlock, *Conium maculatum*, was the classical suicide plant and it is said to have been given to Socrates. Those who did not die of it considered Hemlock was a clean killer as it attacked the body rather than the mind and left the victim to observe his own progressive deterioration. Hemlock is mentioned in Anglo-Saxon medicine, as early as the tenth century, and its principal alkaloid, coniine, is still used.

In small doses it is sedative and anti-spasmodic, and was formerly prescribed against rabies. Effects are contrary to those of strychnine. Poisonous doses cause loss of speech, then of breathing, but without impairing the mental faculties. Irregular heart beats, convulsions and foaming at the mouth end in total paralysis. It is the green plant that is dangerous; dried, it loses much of its poison. For such deadly poison, the plant looks innocuous. It is about four feet high with light greyish-green parsley-like leaves and a few purple blotches on the stem. From the stems the mediaeval herbalists produced the sedative.

Cuckoo-pint, *Arum maculatum*, was as noticeable to us when we arrived on Steep Holm in the 1970s as it had been to Thomas Clark in 1831. A food plant of the Middle Ages, its dried tubers were regarded as aphrodisiac, and also used as a substitute for arrowroot. Clark wrote: "The bright coral berries of the cuckoo-pint were in some spots very conspicuous and ornamental, the plant growing not singly or by twos or threes, as on hedge-banks, but in groups of a dozen or more." It is there now in the same profusion, amongst a carpet of ivy, below the central incline of the track sloping up from the beach. An amazing quantity, exceeding a hundred, smothers the shallow peaty earth that has accumulated beneath the sycamores on the concrete pad to the north of Cliff Cottage.

As a medicinal herb it used to be valued, as a violent purgative and against ring-worm, though it is potentially poisonous. The roots are edible, if properly treated, and were grown for this purpose on the Isle of Portland, Dorset, under the name Portland Sago or Portland Arrowroot. It was a very common starch in former times, and also had cosmetic uses for women – being said to remove freckles.

This short-list of seven island species is advanced here as the cumulative evidence that unusual plants were brought to the island by man. The feature they have in common is that they were used in mediaeval times either as food or medicine. There are many other small plants on the island that also have a pharmacopic pedigree, but from those already described, the point is surely made.

It only remains to be added that Privet was introduced to the island, perhaps even in Roman times though again the monks are more likely to have brought it, and was noticeable enough to receive a mention in the 1625 Norton Beauchamp account-book references to the island. As I often have to remind visitors, it is "Real" Privet, *Ligustrum vulgare*, now ousted from suburban hedges by an Asian substitute. The usurper has larger, softer leaves. The native species has greyish-green leaves and is smothered with sickly white flowers in the spring and masses of black berries in the autumn.

Thomas Clark observed in 1831 that it was the major Steep Holm plant: "The most abundant, at least the one which occupies the largest spaces, is the common privet which closely covers whole acres." Indeed it still does, from the Priory westwards along the southern side of the top of the island, and well down the cliffs in places, as far as Split Rock.

Though John Gerard recommends Privet as a throat gargle,

its presence on Steep Holm seems much more likely to be because of its value as a hedging plant. The Priory garden, in particular, would have needed protection from the wind, and Gerard does not mention its use as a hedge.

Similarly the Elder, *Sambucus niger* has its mention in the Norton Beauchamp lists of 1625, but it could well have arrived on the island in a bird-dropping. The twisted and contorted Steep Holm specimens often stand in superb craggy situations but despite appearances the plant does not achieve great age. In 1831, Thomas Clark saw only a single Elder bush – "under a rock not far from the well" – in the north-east corner of the island. Elder still stands around the same point today, and it was probably from here that cuttings were taken to start shelter-belts along the stone walls that run from the farmsteads across the eastern interior of the island. Ageing Elders grow from ruined walls across the island, and in many places from the cliffs as well.

Because of its fast growth, Elder has been used as a hedging tree since ancient times. It is also among the most useful of all plants. It yields three colours of dye (black, green and purple) and has countless culinary uses (including a pickle from the peeled green shoots) and medicinal ones. The bark is purgative, a fact mentioned by the father of medicine, Hippocrates. The roots are emetic. Ointments of the leaves are emollient and especially good in the treatment of swellings. Elder-flower water is mildly astringent and still used in eye lotion. It was a standard feature of every Victorian lady's dressing table as a skin cleanser, since it whitens and softens the complexion. In mediaeval times it was also widely used against eruptive diseases like measles and also in treating chest complaints. Various preparations of the fruit – as wine, "rob", and syrup – have been used at the onset of influenza and to combat other fevers. Throughout Europe the Elder was regarded as the "medicine chest of the poor" and it is probably the single most important species in general herbal medicine.

OPPOSITE. **Monks' Well: the island's monastic water supply, which was given a steel top by the Royal Engineers in 1941. Lying beneath an elder tree, it became covered by an active scree-slope, immediately above the cliff-face at the north-east corner of the island. Seen from the east on being rediscovered, after a ton of loose stones had been cleared, with Gary Cabell (left) and Philip Howell inspecting. Photographed by Colin Graham in 1976.**

Time-warp: the mediaeval Priory of St Michael emerged as substantial skeleton of footings from the excavations of the 1980s. The inner corner of an L-shaped building is visible (above). Seen from the north-east. Photographed by Colin Graham in 1984.

Crumbling walls: rooms at the west end of the excavated Priory, being the top of the 'L' — note the stones of a monastic grave in the central foreground. Seen from the north-east. Photographed by Rodney Legg in 1992.

Rabbit warreners

When the monks deserted Steep Holm they left at least one usable building. The next occupants of the Priory, perhaps from around 1270 and certainly through the following century, were the rabbit warreners. Their huge midden of rabbit bones mixed with vast numbers of limpet shells was meticulously excavated by Joan Rendell in 1984-89. It had been dumped inside the Priory, forming a pile which had compacted to a depth of more than two feet in the north-western corner of the building. Amongst the limpets were masses of dermal scales of *Raja clavata*, the Thornback Ray, which must have been an important component of the mediaeval diet.

Associated finds at the Priory have included a bronze needle, probably for repairing fishing nets, and a barbed fish-hook with an integral lead weight. Such finds are impossible to date with any precision but the midden also revealed a worn farthing of Edward III [reigned 1327-77] which can be dated to the period 1361-69.

As for the rabbits, they would have been introduced by the Augustinian monks. The religious houses had strong French connections and the rabbit was brought across the English Channel a century after the Battle of Hastings. Even that fact requires stressing. For when I was editing Richard Hattatt's textbook on *Ancient and Romano-British Brooches* I found an obvious representation of a hare, which was a Celtic cult animal, with a statement that it was a rabbit. When I pointed out the error the author was reluctant to accept my alteration because the offending word had come from "the British Museum expert".

Not that the Plantagenets or mediaeval Britons knew the other species, *Oryctolagus cuniculus*, as the rabbit. It was, as numerous documents and hundreds of minor placenames of woods, farms and fields prove, known as the cony or coney or a dozen other versions of the spelling. The name is from the old French "conil" or "conin", deriving from the Latin "cuniculus", which is now its specific scientific name.

The term rabbit would be applied, until the eighteenth century, solely to the young of the coney. The *Promptorium Parvulorum* of 1440 defines a "rabet" as a "yonge conye" and the *Boke of St Albans* in 1486 mentions "conis" as the adults, "bery" as the burrow, and "nest of rebettis" as the young.

In case there are any lingering doubts that the rabbit may

have found its way to Britain before the Normans it can be pointed out that there is no word for it in any of the Celtic or Anglo-Saxon languages or dialects nor is there a single mention of rabbit warrens in the Domesday Book of 1086. The earliest reference that has been found to rabbits in the British Isles is to "de cuniculis" of the Scilly Isles on which Richard de Wyka had not paid tithes, prior to 1176, "believing that tithes were not payable on things of this sort". That phrase itself implies novelty. Further up this coast, at the mouth of the Bristol Channel, the tenant of Lundy Island had the right to take fifty rabbits annually from certain of the "chovis" – coves, perhaps – on the island. That is dated to between 1183 and 1219. By 1225 there was a "custod cuniculorum" – a rabbit warrener – at Bowcombe in the Isle of Wight.

Yet on the English mainland there are no mentions of the rabbit at this time, in forest and hunting permits and other such documents where animals were listed. Archaeologically, the earliest rabbit bones to be dated from an English site are those from Rayleigh Castle, Essex, which was a royal castle from 1163 to 1215. So far nothing has been found to suggest there were any rabbits in Britain before the Plantagenet King Henry II [reigned 1154-89]. The little creatures may well have been brought by returning Crusaders.

One of the earliest documented rabbit warrens in Plantagenet England was on Brean Down which was then effectively an island. Islands provided an easy way of isolating the newly introduced animals and preventing their escape. An added advantage was that islands were free from ground predators such as foxes, weasels, stoats and polecats. Elspeth M. Veale concludes in the *Agricultural Historical Review* of 1957 that "the rabbit became established in the late twelfth century on the small islands off the English coast". Later, in "the middle years of the thirteenth century coneygarths were being more widely set up on the mainland, but even late in the century rabbits were to be found only on certain estates".

Ingenious methods were devised for catching the warrened rabbits, including circular stone-walled enclosures of prime sheltered grazing land in the generally windswept Shetlands. These compounds filled with rabbits after a stone had been removed from the entrance. The lush grass proved to be their last supper as the stone was stealthily replaced. In Norfolk, where all the grass was green but the ground was much easier to dig, a deep pit was excavated and covered with a wooden trap-door. Nothing has yet been found to show how the Steep

Holm rabbits were trapped but it is likely to have been a version of the Shetland technique.

Rabbits had a double value as a commodity, being sold either for their skins, their meat, or for both. Those being killed on Lundy in 1272 fetched 5 shillings 6 pence per hundred skins "because the flesh is not sold". Those for meat were sixpence each when the Abbot of St Austin's Abbey held a banquet at Canterbury in 1309; though he could have shopped around and bought ten for a shilling in Oxford market in 1310. They were 2 pence in Farnham, Surrey, but 7 pence plus a halfpenny for transport at Bushey, Hertfordshire.

These prices, and the fact that Lundy's meat from an annual cull of two thousand was uneconomic to bring to market, suggest a pronounced west to east rise in their value. The west, with its islands, seems to have been the general area where they were farmed in quantity for their skins. Further east, to eat, they were regarded as a luxury food and priced accordingly. They had the status of being a royal dish and were consumed in quantity at feasts and banquets, such as those for coronations and the appointment of archbishops. Four thousand rabbits were purchased for the celebratory feast that followed the enthronement of the Archbishop of York in 1465.

John Russell's 1460 *Book of Nurture* gives instructions for cooking and carving of young rabbit. Regarding "the cony, lay him on the back in the dish, if he have grease" and then "unlace that cony".

By 1492 there were rabbits thriving on Flat Holm. There was a problem, however, on Steep Holm. The following mention of the Steep Holm rabbits occurs in the account books of the manor of Norton Beauchamp for 1625. I have modernised the spellings:

"There be also within the said island certain grey conies, in the number of twenty or thirty couples by estimation, but of no value, because by experience had of them, they be so fed with garlic, privet and elder (grass lacking) that they do savour of the garlic and privet in eating."

The mediaeval taste for strong foods was already sliding into bland mediocrity before the English Civil War. The "garlicke" of the note is the Wild Leek. Another timeless thing is the remark in parenthesis about the absence of grass.

Scientifically, the most interesting observation about the Steep Holm rabbits occurs in one of the nineteenth century books about this coast. John Rutter writes in his *Deliniations of the North-West Division of the County of Somerset* in 1829: "A few rabbits continue to exist on the rock, whose fur is of a redder cast than rabbits usually have." Here is a general topographical writer, thirty years before Wallace and Darwin, noticing that colonies of animals isolated from the mainstream of their kind tend to develop different characteristics, or as in this case to preserve an older strain. He did not express it that way, but he recorded the relevant fact.

W.G.M. Jones, who was serving on the island in 1943, speaks of the "small reddish-brown rabbits" maintaining a "precarious existence". J.W. Hunt, who visited Steep Holm in about 1955, recalled that the rabbits were "red behind the ears, like the Belgian hare". On 23 August 1975, Robert Spiller, who had made a large number of visits to the island, spotted the same coloration on a rabbit near Laboratory Battery. This characteristic, usually orange rather than red, is now seen in only a minority of the Steep Holm rabbits.

Their numbers have been brought almost to the point of extinction since Dr Armand Delille inoculated a pair of rabbits with the virus *Myxomatosis cuniculus* and released them into the countryside west of Paris in June 1952. Some have said that the culprits for the last stage of its journey to Steep Holm were the gulls, bringing food for their young, but according to Dorothy Crampton of the former Steep Holm Trust the disease was introduced deliberately in 1955. Rabbit numbers on the island have fluctuated wildly since. In 1967 the island rabbit population was estimated at 250 and there were several new warrens. Fifty-four rabbits were caught and marked (sixteen of them being captured twice). Five of the total were already tagged, having been trapped the previous year.

The numbers were still relatively high in 1975. One night, between gull catching and ringing, the Cardiff University team led by Dr Peter Ferns counted nearly twenty rabbits. In daytime they were keeping to the dense scrub areas because those animals that came into the open were vulnerable to attack from the omnipresent colony of gulls. Young rabbits that had not learned this rule were frequently found dead and mutilated beside the island paths through the early and middle parts of the summer.

The favourite habitat was at the edge of the scrub-belt northeast of the Barracks which fringed the remnants of the old gull-lawns. Here they often gnaw the lower stems of the Alexanders, sometimes toppling the plants. Many of the rabbits dig underground burrows but others may live on the surface. It is arguable whether myxomatosis particularly attacks those living in burrows and also debatable whether its presence on the island is enzootic. The alternative theory is that the virulent attacks that periodically devastate the colony are caused by reinfection from diseased fragments of dead rabbits brought from the mainland by gulls.

Each recurrence is of similar severity and wipes out eighty to ninety per cent of the colony. Such is their proverbial capacity for breeding that the recovery will take only a couple of years.

'Nature, red in tooth and claw': a Steep Holm rabbit, spared myxomatosis and instead caught in its prime by visiting predator Salman Legg. It provoked strong reactions from at least one human, displaying in a further line from Tennyson 'The blind hysterics of the Celt'. Only vegetarians have the right to take offence — for each of our species commissions far worse every day. Photographed by Rodney Legg in 1990.

Port of Bristol limits

By the twelfth century, the city of Bristol had become the most flourishing port in England, next to London, and the capital's recognition of the fact came in 1373 with the granting of a charter by Edward III. This made Bristol a distinct county and set its boundaries to include the deep-water channel down the Severn estuary for some twenty miles from Avonmouth. The south-western limit of this jurisdiction was the island of Steep Holm which formed the last natural marker before the open sea.

An actual stone was placed on the island, and its successor is a 60 cm high slab of grey Pennant sandstone, shaped like a small milestone with a rounded top. This stone was placed on the island beach as part of the city's celebrations for Queen Victoria's diamond jubilee. "C.B. 1897", it is inscribed, the letters standing for the City and County of Bristol. As for its second-city port status, this had been lost to Liverpool in the eighteenth century, and the position of the present stone is both a theoretical and a physical puzzle.

Firstly, it does not coincide at all with the boundary of Bristol as it is laid down, as required by law, in the administrative maps of the Ordnance Survey. These show the Bristol boundary – which is also the corner of its sea-going Southville ward – as not reaching the beach area at all. The point at which it touches the island is on the north side, at the mean low water line a third of the way along the rocky shore between the Hall Cave promontory and 208 Steps Searchlight Post. Nowhere along that shore is accessible at high water and the beach must have seemed a welcome alternative.

The second problem with the location of the stone is that no one can see it. Since the building of the quay wall, by the Royal Engineers in 1941, it has been invariably covered by shingle. It is also doubly overhung, firstly by a great slab of wartime concrete, and then by the natural projection of the cliff.

Michael Yesson uncovered it in 1976, in order to re-key the slab of concrete into the cliff, and it was visible for an hour. Chris Maslen saw it again, for about the same length of time, in 1987. He was then re-building the beach steps into their present form. These are further forward from the older block of concrete and the cliff overhang, and the stone is now covered with two metres or more of pebbles.

For the sake of the record, it lies beneath the overhang at a point 1.5 metres west from the edge of the top step.

Island owners

It is a complicated, and probably impossible, matter to unravel the precise mediaeval ownership of Steep Holm, or its alleged ownership for the matter was at times contested between aristocratic tenants and at other periods tenants stopped paying rent and claimed to have assumed ownership. These seem to have been its owners from 1086 to 1461:

1. Walter de Dowai (at the time of the 1086 Domesday Survey)
2. Harold de Ewias (alive in 1100; was tenant to de Dowai in his lands in north Somerset)
3. Robert de Ewyas (Harold's son)
4. Robert de Ewyas (Robert's son; alive in 1210)
5. Sybil, wife of Robert de Tregoz (she was Robert's daughter)
6. Geoffrey de Tregoz (their son)
7. Robert de Tregoz (Geoffrey's son; alive in 1265)
8. John, Baron Tregoz (left only daughters)
9. a member of the Bec family of Eresby, Linconshire (by another of Robert's children, via marriage, in the 1270s)
10. Thomas de Bec (Bishop of St David's, died in 1293)
10a. Robert de Berkeley (tenant for life; reverted to Thomas)
11. John de Bec (brother of Thomas)
12. Henry de Laci, Earl of Lincoln (granted by John between 1307-22)
13. Sir Thomas de Berkeley (via the island's tenant, Walter de Burcey, who relinquished his rights in Sir Thomas's favour)
14. Sir Maurice Berkeley
15. Sir Thomas Berkeley (alive 1418)
16. James Butler, fourth Earl of Ormonde (possibly after a dispute over the Berkeleys' alleged title; died 1452)
17. James Butler, fifth Earl of Ormonde and Earl of Wiltshire (James's son, 1420-61, would become Lord High Treasurer of England but was captured by the Yorkists after the Battle of Towton and beheaded)
18. The Crown (in 1461, as a result of the forfeiture of James's estates).

The next strand that I have picked up is that the island was among the colossal list of properties that were owned by Edward Seymour, first Earl of Hertford and Duke of Somerset [?1506-52], who would be another of its distinguished owners to lose his head. When he was Protector of England his estates were managed by his devoted friend Sir John Thynne of Longleat, which would lead to the island providing some appropriate avian fauna to enliven the family's Wiltshire grounds in 1587. Seymour's eldest son, Sir Edward Seymour, Earl of Hertford [?1539-1621] was prevented from inheriting the title Duke of Somerset, and it would pass on to William Seymour, first Marquis and second Earl of Hertford [1588-1660] to become the second Duke of Somerset. His name graces a famous royal romance: at the age of fifteen he captivated Lady Arabella Stuart, and would be seen by Charles the First as a useful pawn when the war clouds thickened. He was appointed Lord Lieutenant of Somerset in 1639 and survived a series of Civil War battles to do his master one last service in arranging for the beheaded king to be buried at Windsor. Seymour survived just long enough to be on the quayside to welcome Charles II at Dover on 26 May 1660.

His successor, in contrast, had only a brief life, though it does provide a Steep Holm footnote. At Michaelmas in 1670, the bailiff for William Seymour, third Duke of Somerset [succeeded 1651, died 1671] rented Steep Holm to "Russell of South Brent village" for an annual rent of ten shillings plus twenty Berrow ducks.

John Seymour, the fourth Duke of Somerset, died in 1675 and Francis Seymour, the fifth Duke, was murdered near Genoa in 1678. Charles Seymour, the sixth Duke of Somerset [1662-1748], became known as the "Proud Duke" for his behaviour to kings, servants and wives alike.

On the death of Algernon Seymour, the seventh Duke of Somerset [1684-1750] there were no direct male heirs and a great dispersion followed of titles and estates. The Dukedom went to a grandson, Sir Edward Seymour [1695-1757] but I am unsure what had become of the matter of the island ownership. It turns up again in a deed of 1786 as part of a large Somerset holding owned by John Freke Willes of Northamptonshire. The "messuage or tenement ... now standing" on the island was in the occupation of Thomas Yateman, though he was probably an absentee tenant. I will resume the matter of ownership in the section on its elaborate 1832 improvements scheme.

Gulls for Longleat

I have mentioned the Steep Holm connection with Longleat House, Wiltshire, one of the grandest mansions in the country, the creation of which had been Sir John Thynne's life's work. The enhancement of its landscape had been interrupted by his death in 1580. In 1578, a series of small ponds were constructed in the grounds.

A consignment of 96 gulls were obtained from Steep Holm for the purpose, the estate's historian David Burnett told me, of tethering beside the water to give it a maritime flavour. He found the following entry in the vellum ledgers for 1578:

"To a servant of Mr Paynes bringing from Steepholmes VIII doz gulls . . . 2s."

They could not have been acquired for eating as there are a series of subsequent entries that provide for their welfare and feeding. These, typically, read:

"To Mistress Spycer for offal for ye gulls . . . 9d."

Thus, in an unexpectedly high-class document, the bird for which Steep Holm would become notorious makes its entry into the historical record. Gulls and Steep Holm have been synonymous for at least four centuries.

Channel shipping: Victorian model of a sailing barge, rescued by Jenny Smith from its watery grave at the bottom of the Farmhouse catchment-tank. Photographed by Rodney Legg in 1992.

Captain Kidd's treasure

Legends take on a life of their own and the silly story that has caused intrusions over the years to the island's archaeology and wildlife is the persistent belief that Captain Kidd's treasure is buried there. I do point out the improbability factor, which is that we are talking about burying the largely perishable contents of a merchant ship on a solid rock that has barely two inches of soil, but that is not something that the press will report. Or the the fact that although the pirate William Kidd was hanged at Wapping in 1701, he seems to have hidden the loot from the *Queda Merchant*, which was sailing under French colours, on Gardiners Island at the mouth of Long Island Sound. That is some way off Weston-super-Mare.

The Daily Telegraph did, however, quote me on 21 May 1990 saying that the treasure hunters had targeted Steep Holm for special attention:

"People are coming ashore very regularly, all convinced they are going to dig up Captain Kidd's treasure. They will be shown the sea at the end of a sharp stick whenever I catch them. It has got so bad that nesting sites are being disturbed and genuine archaeological digs damaged by these idiots with their metal detectors."

That is not to say that Captain Kidd never stepped ashore on Steep Holm. Many mariners have done so, to pick up pilots or await the tide before continuing up the estuary, and then as now – as the intelligence officers of HM Customs and Excise realise – it is an excellent place for secreting something for later recovery.

THE DAILY TELEGRAPH, MONDAY, MAY 21, 1990

Island plundered

By Paul Stokes

TREASURE hunters have been warned against plundering an island nature reserve which has already been ravaged by storms in the Bristol Channel.

Steep Holm, off Weston-super-Mare, is proving to be an increasing attraction for visitors armed with metal detectors who have been blamed for disturbing the wildlife.

Mr Rodney Legg, warden of the island run by the Allsop Trust, said interest had been fuelled by recent publications about the legend of Captain Kidd with cryptic references to buried treasure.

"People are coming ashore very regularly, all convinced they are going to dig up Captain Kidd's treasure," he said. "They will all be shown the sea at the end of a sharp stick whenever I catch them.

"It has got so bad that nesting sites are being disturbed and genuine archaeological digs damaged by these idiots with their metal detectors."

He added: "The legends about the islands and pirates and smugglers date from Victorian romantic fiction.

"Now new books are coming out hinting about treasure on Steep Holm and Flat Holm, but there is no evidence that Captain Kidd ever came here."

98

The explorers

I have outlined, in the section on the monastic flora, how the key mediaeval plant introductions were rediscovered by a succession of explorers. The first scholarly visitor was William Turner, the Dean of Wells [died 1568] who had written a herbal in 1546, though its publication was delayed until 1551 when it appeared as *A newe Herball wherein are conteyned the names of Herbs*. It was the start of scientific botany in this country, and in the course of his work in the Wells diocese he took the opportunity of a boat journey to Steep Holm in the 1550s.

It led to the first recorded mention of the former pot-herb Alexanders growing in wild profusion in "Ilandes compassed about the sea". This appears in *The Seconde Parte of W.T.'s Herball*. I am hoping that some researcher may find more in the diocesan records, or in a further search of the additions to the supplement which Turner proceeded to resume after inserting a treatise with the sub-title *Hereunto is joined a booke of the bath of Baeth*.

This shows a delightful respect for the sanctity of knowledge, that it might be slipped in wherever the opportunity of printing occurred, and it shows a grasp of the spontaneity and excitement of the medium that we have lost by bringing to it the conventions demanded by closed minds. Here mine would like to make the point by giving you a dissertation on what lies beyond the universe. "A brick wall," I've just been told. That's the trouble with science today – it knows everything.

As for the Steep Holm explorers, the next was the physician James Newton [1639-1718] whose dates I have taken from information provided by Professor William T. Stearn, as those in the *Dictionary of National Biography* [?1664-1750] do not tie in with the naturalist John Ray knowing from Newton, by 1668, that the Wild Leek was growing on Steep Holm. It does not seem likely that there was another botanically minded James Newton who searched out Steep Holm, particularly as the one of the *Dictionary* is said by the botanist Leonard Plukenet [1642-1706] to have scoured the country as "Stirpium Britannicarum explorator indefessus".

There was some kind of resumed island occupation about this time. The archaeological team's work on the post-mediaeval midden in the west end of the former Priory revealed a total of seventy-two fragments of a tripod-pitcher, in gravel-tempered Devon ware. The pot is dated to around 1650.

What Newton did for Britain, Joseph Banks [1743-1820] was doing for the world in 1771 and his rôle as Captain Cook's plant-collector has eclipsed his July 1773 boat ride to Steep Holm. He was accompanied by the naturalist Rev John Lightfoot [1735-88]. I am hoping, however, that some descriptive record has survived of their day on the island, though the archivist at Kew Gardens – itself a creation of Sir Joseph Banks – assures me that there is no relevant diary entry. All we have is a list of his discoveries on the island. Banks was the first to record the following as Steep Holm plants – Sea Spleenwort, Tree Mallow, Sea Storksbill, Hemlock, Rock Samphire, Caper Spurge and Golden Samphire.

Discovery of the Wild Peony was delayed, my explanation being that previous visitors did not come to the island until after it had flowered, until the arrival of F.P. Wright in 1803. This coincided with the great flourish of Romantic Movement enthusiasm for the wild beauties of England. Things natural and rustic were in vogue and the pioneer poet of the age celebrated Steep Holm in verses that compare its wild, rugged terrain with the splendour of a flower that would look more in place in a living room vase.

William Lisle Bowles [1762-1850], a clergyman, penned the lines featuring the island of Steep Holm and its unexpected treasure. It is a place that "abrupt and high" ...

"And desolate and cold, and bleak, uplifts
Its barren brow-barren, but on its steep
One native flower is seen, the peony;
One flower, which smiles in sunshine or in storm,
There sits companionless, but yet not sad."

He makes the inevitable moral comparison,
which is that:
". . . so Virtue, a fair flower
Blooms on the rock of Care, and, though unseen,
So smiles in cold seclusion."

Bowles was hailed by Wordsworth, Coleridge and Southey for reviving natural poetry and indeed Wordsworth and his cliché daffodils seem yet more trite after reading what William Lisle Bowles managed with the Wild Peony. His sonnet put the island on the menu for visitors, and its special plant became endangered. A party of so-called scientists are said to have nearly eradicated the famous Wild Peony in 1834.

William Withering [1775-1832] visited Steep Holm in June 1826 when he was revising his father's *British Plants* for its seventh edition. He found what must have been the old Priory garden, a "little enclosure with ruinous walls and few remaining vestiges", on the site that would be obliterated by the Garden Battery. He says that no inhabitant had dwelt upon the island "within the memory of man" save "the solitary fisherman who makes the crazy hut his cheerless abode, and that only through the dreary season of winter".

Thomas Clark, a Somerset botanist, was typical of those tempted by the island's fame and he made the trip to Steep Holm in 1831. "I have had for many years the wish to visit the island," he wrote, "principally on account of the rare plants which grow there – the Piony, the Great Round-headed Garlic, and the Caper Spurge. We found them all there and I have them now planted in my garden."

"The Piony" was the Wild Peony and "Great Round-headed Garlic" a perfectly descriptive name for the Wild Leek. Much to his excitement, Clark recognised the latter from the sea.

"The garlic I saw and knew from the boat before we landed, growing abundantly on a high ridge at the eastern end of the island, though I know not that I ever saw it before." Here, below Tower Rock (then called Lion's Head) the Wild Leek was still growing in profusion, amongst clumps of Wild Peony, during the first World War. It was from there that Tony Parsons and I rescued bulbs that had rolled on to the rocks below, and set about the task of helping the plant to re-colonise the higher cliffs. Indeed we had noted the globes of pink flower from the sea during our August visits of 1974-77.

By that time in 1831, Thomas Clark found that the Alexanders had died back into their dry, stalky state. "The foliage being nearly decayed," he could bring home only some seeds and roots, but made a useful assessment of their status on the island: "This was very plentiful, I think all over the island; I distinctly recollect it at both ends."

Those words have been echoed over the years by a growing number of non-botanists who have seemed somewhat unimpressed by the island's ecological monoculture.

Explorers still search out Steep Holm when the Wild Peony is in flower, though usually they book their trips after reading of its flowering dates from books and fail to take global warming into effect. The only petals that Caroline, Duchess of Beaufort, saw on her visit, on 12 May 1990, were lying on the ground. Botanical artist Lys de Bray, from Wimborne in Dorset, had more luck in the 1970s when the wind started blowing and she was stranded, alone on the island and painting the Peony, in a glass of water in the Barracks, for forty-eight hours longer than she had expected. "They were the happiest two days of my life," she recalled for 'The Natural History Programme" on Radio 4 in 1990.

The globe trotter Bruce Chatwin [1940-89] whose skill with terse disconnected sentences was to stir them into an atmosphere glittering like a Byzantine mosaic – to paraphrase Andrew Sinclair of The Times – comes to Steep Holm on page 344 of *What I am Doing Here*. That was in 1977: "My companion was a naturalist in his eighties. The purpose of our visit was to see in flower the peony that is supposed to have been brought here as a medicinal herb by monks from the Mediterranean."

In the book Steep Holm is then immediately upstaged by Hermaness, "the ultimate headland of the British Isles" at "the tip of Unst in Shetland". It has an albatross, and on hearing that at nine o'clock in the evening Chatwin packs his bags and makes it to King's Cross for the night sleeper to Aberdeen. Two days later he has the bird in his binoculars; which has little to do with Steep Holm except that Colin Graham insists Chatwin came to the island with his friend Salman Rushdie, sightings of whom are now at a premium.

Salman my cat, given his name in 1988 before the Iatollah's fatwah, does visit the island. It is his only experience of freedom because at home that is compromised, at the end of a lead, to thwart his natural desire for playing with cars on the A303. I have on occasion complained that the island attracts only the aged, white and middle class but it might be of some reassurance to the other Salman that there is a general absence of Iranian visitors. Colin's memory is that Salman the libertarian was on Steep Holm on 10 May 1977, a date of some consequence to the former as his thirtieth birthday. I have my doubts, but that applies to most things.

Botanical artist: Lys de Bray, whose two days on Steep Holm were 'the happiest of my life'. Photographed by Colin Graham in 1973.

OPPOSITE. Standing in the garden: the site of the monastery garden with John Pitfield in the Victorian western barbette at Garden Battery. 1941-erected Royal Artillery range-finding pill behind, with plaque to pre-war warden Harry Cox. Seen from the east. Photographed by Rodney Legg in 1991.

Shelter from the storm?

A rectangular Tenement was built to the north-west of the Priory in 1776. The ruin is 10 metres long by 4.5 metres wide with walls that are built directly on the topsoil – a fact I discovered when I underpinned the collapsing south-east corner – and stand to a height of 2.2 metres. There are fireplaces at each end.

It was ostensibly built as a refuge for fishermen, stranded on the island by storms, which not only indicates consistency in the English weather but shows that at the time the island was uninhabited. The inference is that the Priory was also beyond economic repair, though the end furthest from the Tenement would be re-roofed in 1866 as a foreman's hut, and the new work must have re-used much of the stone from its western half.

The effort required even for a building of this modest scale would have been considerable on an island and shows there was an economic motive for providing such facilities. But for what? Boatmen show little inclination to become builders and being accustomed to a cramped cabin they can survive in an emergency in a space of less than forty-five square metres. Once on a fifty acre island they would no longer be in imminent danger.

There is a more plausible explanation of the type of persons who would require some home comforts during an enforced wait.

OPPOSITE. **Phoney excuse: not a refuge for victims of shipwreck, but of eighteenth century free-traders, otherwise known as smugglers. The ruins of the Tenement, built in 1776 and lying north-west of the Priory. Seen from the west, with the flak-top of the 6-inch 1941-built gun battery at Garden Battery East being glimpsed in the distance (centre right). Photographed by Colin Graham in 1976.**

Smugglers' cave

Fifty metres south-west of the Tenement, on the cliff-edge overlooking the South Landing, lies the reason for its existence. It is the little arched cave, known as Parsons Cave, which has the remains of walling across its entrance that has identical mortar to that of the Tenement. So secreted is this spot that even with all the exploring that took place on the island in the second half of the twentieth century it was not re-discovered until 1985.

As I have noted in the geological section, the cave itself is two metres high and 2.5 metres deep. It is 3.6 metres wide at the entrance with a wall that is now three stones high at the west end and six stones high at the opposite end. A slipped stone partially blocks the entrance which is otherwise 68 cm wide.

Stan and Joan Rendell have pointed out in the *Steep Holm Magazine* for 1985 that with the displaced stone removed the gap "would provide better access for someone carrying a brandy keg".

Smuggling was the great illicit trade of the eighteenth and early nineteenth centuries and only the failures are documented. The Rendells quote Rev John Ashley, the founder of the Bristol Channel Mission, for a diary entry at the end of the smuggling era. It is dated 28 March 1843, but was of an occurrence that would have been commonplace half a century earlier:

" . . . a landing of brandy was effected on the island a short time since, advantage being taken of its lonely situation to introduce and keep it in the rocks there till opportunity admitted of its being conveyed to the mainland."

The island's rôle would have been as a place of refuge if the weather or efforts of the Customs and Excise service made a direct landing on the mainland inadvisable. The cave in question is about 185 feet above the South Landing, a height which would not have precluded the hauling of kegs by rope, and was probably reached by an offshoot from the mediaeval South Landing path which has been cut through by the incline of 1866 and is generally in a landslipped condition.

The cave could well have seen use, for human habitation, long before in the mediaeval period, as an anchorite's cell. Given the island's monastic associations it is likely to have attracted religious hermits.

OPPOSITE. **Anchorite's cell or smugglers' cave: or indeed both, the author believes. Parsons Cave, with remains of walling, being visited by Salman Legg. Seen from the south. Photographed by Rodney Legg in 1991.**

Harvesting the gulls

The fishermen of the upper Bristol Channel used to carry out an annual slaughter of the gulls on Steep Holm. Their eggs were sold to Bristol companies that refined sugar-cane, which was imported from the Caribbean, and the mass killing of the chicks of the gulls, and other sea-birds, was to produce down for bedding and cushions.

Henry Farr Yeatman of Stock House, near Lydlinch, in Dorset, had shot a gull from the slopes of Brent Knoll, when he was a boy. It disgorged "at least a pint of large earthworms" as it died. The moment was recalled on 1 January 1817 when he completed his poem *Brent Knoll*. Lines on the gulls chart their flight across the hill towards their haunts in mid-Channel:

> Now from the marsh, and fallow field, and hill
> With worms, and insects laden to the full
> Comes the long struggling team of screaming gulls
> Returning homeward, to their haunts for rest,
> With weary wings and in strange harmony
> Making such concert as I love to hear.

Yeatman also records, in a footnote, the reality of human predation upon the island's gull colony:

"On the steep Holmes in the middle of the Channel, millions of these birds, of every species, build their nests in the summer months; the fisherman at this time with a long pole armed with a noose at the end climbs to the edge of the cliff where they are sitting, and having uttered a peculiar cry to excite the bird's attention, and which causes it to thrust out its neck, throws the loop with great dexterity over the bird's neck, and with one twitch jerks it into the boat beneath where his family are waiting to strip it in a moment of its feathers, and to commit its body to the deep. The eggs are sold by boatloads to the Bristol merchants for the purpose of refining sugar."

OPPOSITE. **Ready for plucking: a gull chick ripe for the harvest, to provide down for pillows and cushions. This one, however, was among Rodney Legg's pets and lived to get airborne, from a nest beside the rebuilt Inn. Photographed by the Bristol Evening Post in 1992.**

Shipwrecks

The *Rebecca*, a West India company merchantman, was wrecked on Steep Holm in 1810. She was homeward bound, coming into Bristol with a cargo of rum, and that had been spirited away by the time H M Customs and Excise service arrived to examine the wreckage.

Then on 23 October 1817 the *William and Mary*, a packet boat, was in desperate difficulties off "the Holm lighthouse, Bristol Channel". She seems to have struck the Wolves rocks, a mile north-west from Flat Holm, though another account gives the obstacle as "the Willeys". At any event she went down in foul conditions with nearly sixty lives.

Steep Holm was untouched by the Napoleonic wars and its cannon from that period would be brought across much later in the nineteenth century, as pivots for larger guns when war nerves broke out again in the 1860s.

WESTERN DAILY PRESS, SATURDAY, JANUARY 23, 1993

The Government has a duty to revitalise the economy, but it is up to employers to capitalise on this with the best possible workforce — based on talent, not age.

125 YEARS AGO

One boatman drowned and another went adrift after the men lost their way in dense fog while returning to Weston-super-Mare from Steep Holme. The survivor endured extreme cold and went without food and water until a French vessel rescued him three days later.

THOUGHT FOR THE DAY

The Lord taketh pleasure in them that fear him, in those that hope in his mercy.

Psalm 147:11

Proof of a private beach

"The Steep Holmes, property to be sold or let," ran an advertisement in the Bristol Mirror of 9 June 1827. "The Steep Holmes and Fishery in the Bristol Channel," was offered by A. Murray, a surveyor and land agent of 61 St Martin's Lane in central London – who specialised in upper-crust estates. His additional information about the island is important as it shows, despite a paucity of information that was to hand when John Fowles and I signed the island's conveyance for the Kenneth Allsop Memorial Trust in 1976, that the island ownership also includes its beach. This is still staked with the remains of a line of nets.

The wording of the advertisement, spotted by Jane Evans of Woodsdpring Museum in 1985, is that the Steep Holm beach and inter-tidal zone is not Crown property, as might otherwise be assumed, but belongs with the island's freehold. Murray – which coincidentally is also the name of the land agent who would sell Steep Holm to the Allsop Trust in 1973-76 – states: "The island has long been celebrated for rabbits and an extensive Salmon and Sprat industry. The Bristol market is mostly supplied with fish caught at this island."

The salmon still cross the island's beach tide-race and jump the pebble bank, as the seals know to their advantage during a traditional late-summer vacation up-Channel to the island from their Welsh breeding grounds. Bristol Channel fishermen of the late twentieth century seem reluctant to admit any similar knowledge.

In the case of the 1827 Mr Murray, he was unsuccessful in finding an immediate buyer, and Steep Holm would remain the property of William Willes until 1830.

OPPOSITE. **Clipping: 'I wondered if you had seen this,' wrote Lloyd McCreadie of Charlton Horethorne, Somerset, who spotted a Steep Holm tragedy from Victorian days resurrected in the Western Daily Press. Dating from the time of the island's fortifications, 1868.**

Thomas Clark's visit

When the botanist Thomas Clark [1793-1864] came to Steep Holm, from Street, on 16 August 1831 he also noted the path clearance that had begun on the eastern cliffs, above the beach landing, though work had not yet begun on the construction either of the Inn or the Cliff Cottage. John Baker had just bought the island and had elaborate plans for its future. Though neither of his proposed buildings is mentioned in Thomas Clark's diary account of the visit, he gives information about improvements being carried out to the cliff path, which had led to the discovery of a shell midden: "Several men were employed in cutting a winding road from the little pebble beach, our landing place, at the eastern end of the island, to the top, in part through solid rock; and in one place they had dug through a bed of shells of the common limpet, mixed only with a little loose earth. It was a query how they came there, and at what remote time. Perhaps, numerous as they are, they are only the accumulated heap thrown from time to time from some cottage or hut, of whose inhabitants this shell fish formed, it may be, the principal food, and though we did not observe any vestige of a building very near, the well of good spring water, the only well on the island, is almost close by."

The account is well worth quoting in full, given that it provides an insight into the current state of botanical and antiquarian knowledge, which would be expanded by another Somerset worthy, John Skinner, a year later. Clark continues by speculating on the origin of those limpet shells:

"Gildas, the historian, appears from Rutter's *Delineations of the North Western Division of the County of Somerset*, to have led a hermit kind of life here, and it may be that his dinners contributed to this accumulation of shells. Githa, the mother of Harold, the last of the Saxon Kings, who also took refuge here, was, I hope supplied with more queenly food.

"The old house on the top of the island, and near the eastern end, has been in part repaired for the accommodation of the workmen. Here we dined off the sandwiches and tarts with which we were provided, in a room which reminded us of the romance descriptions of a cave of banditti. It contained three or four small beds, and the pots, frying-pans and other cooking apparatus of the whole inhabitants of the island. We however were as little disposed to be dissatisfied with our dining-room as with our dinner, and I know not whether we the more enjoyed this repast or our far more elegant tea-supper when we got back to our hotel at Weston.

"I have had for many years the wish to visit this island, principally on account of the rare plants which I know grow there – the piony, the great round-headed garlic, and the caper spurge. We found all three and I have them now planted in my garden. The garlic I saw and knew from the boat before we landed, growing abundantly on a high ridge at the eastern end of the island, though I know not that I ever saw it before. The piony and the spurge grow on the flat top. The shrubby saltwort and the tree mallow, as I have since learnt, are also inhabitants of the island. The latter Dr Gapper tells me he once found there.

"He also informs me that a plant of which I have brought home the seeds and roots only, the foliage being nearly decayed, is the common Alexanders. This was very plentiful, I think, all over the island; I distinctly recollect it at both ends.

"I was much interested with a plant growing on a rocky declivity at the western end, but could not get to it without greater labour and risk than I was disposed to encounter. It appeared to be composed of upright stems a foot or more high, clothed with bright green leaves and covered on the top with golden flowers. Dr Gapper supposed it to be the samphire-leaved flea-bane.

"Besides these there are many other plants of less interest. The most abundant, at least the one which occupies the largest space, is the common privet which closely covers whole acres. It probably forms, as Dr Gapper remarks, the principal food of the numerous rabbits on the island, for though they do not, I believe, usually eat this plant, I do not know what else they can have to live on, at least in the winter. The other plants that I recollect to be in great abundance are ragwort and wood sage.

"Young plants of henbane I observed on the top of the island, near the caper spurge, and a single bush of elder under a rock not far from the well. Ivy grows about the rocks in some places; also the common polypody, wall-rue, spleenwort, wall pelli-tory; samphire plentifully. The bright coral berries of the cuckoo-pint were on some spots very conspicuous and orna-mental, the plant growing not singly or by twos or threes, as on hedgebanks, but in groups of a dozen or more.

"The only butterfly which I recollect to have seen is a large white one, I suppose the large cabbage butterfly. The two very common snails, *Helix aspersa* and *nemoralis*, were very plentiful and fine. A smaller snail, *Helix virgata*, I believe, was also very plentiful, and I found a few empty shells of *Turbo elegans*. *H.*

113

aspersa I have before observed to be commonly of a large size near the sea. Is this from the influence of the sea air, or because that on the sea border it is left to attain its full growth and not destroyed at all ages, as in gardens?"

Such observations on the island's outsized snails would be repeated in the 1970s, and lead to a research project that would confirm not only their largeness, but the "fine" colours that Clark hints at. He also seems to have found the Priory Garden:

"At the south eastern corner of the island near the house there is a space of perhaps 50 yards square which we supposed was once a garden and brother William was strongly of the opinion that piony and other rare plants were once cultivated in it and since its desertion have run wild where they would, an opinion which on the whole I think likely to be correct. This place is surrounded by a ridge of stones which I took for the dilapidated wall, but Robert Anstice, though he is of the opinion that the plants are not indigenous, says it may have been a rude fortification.

"At the western end I observed an oval space, also surrounded with a ridge of stone, but still ruder and less conspicuous." This is the probable Roman signal station at Rudder Rock, that would be first recognised as such, though he thought the beacon was Danish, by John Skinner in 1832.

"The island is far more picturesque than I had supposed it to be. Instead of being the clumpy rock which it appears from the main land, its shores are indented with little bays and varied with projecting and detached rocks, and the sides are traversed by fissures and little ravines. These were richly and profusely ornamented with the golden flowers of the ragwort and in some places the rocks were ornamented almost as richly and profusely with samphire, its lively green leaves being scarcely less bright than the flowers."

OPPOSITE, top. **The Holmes: 'Sketch of the Channel the Steep and Flat Holmes and the coast of Wales.' Seen from the east. Sketched by John Skinner in 1832.**

OPPOSITE, below. **Extremity: described by Skinner as the 'northern' end of Steep Holm, but in fact the western tip of the island with Rudder Rock being depicted (right) and Flat Holm in the background. The wording emerging from the spine of the book is for 'Penarth Point' as the full picture shows the Welsh coast. Seen from the south. Sketched by John Skinner in 1832.**

The coming of Skinner: 'Approach to the Steep Holmes from Weston July 26.' Seen from the east. Sketched by John Skinner in 1832.

On the Rock: 'Monumental Strata above the landing place' which is a view of Tower Rock (right) looking across the water to Brean Down (left) and Brent Knoll (right of centre). Seen from the north-west. Sketched by John Skinner in 1832.

John Skinner's visit

Archaeologically and historically, with enough natural history for all-round credibility, the best single day-and-a-half of research ever carried out on Steep Holm was achieved by Rev John Skinner [1772-1839] on 26-27 July 1832. He gives us hard information about everything from the finds of Roman pottery, the St Gildas associations, and the supposed Danish signal station – like all antiquaries he followed the conventional assumption that oval earthworks had to be Danish – onwards to his present day and the building of an Inn and a harbour on the eastern shore by the new proprietor, John Baker.

Skinner had been curate of South Brent. From September 1800 he had as his own parish, Camerton near Bath, and he set about recording its antiquities. He also studied the origins of the Celtic language. As a local antiquary he was the greatest that Somerset would produce.

In all a total of ninety-eight manuscript volumes, illustrated throughout with watercolour sketches, would be bequeathed to the British Museum on his suicide in October 1839. These volumes are mainly about Somerset, though he did venture across to France and Holland, and they are a superb quarry for twentieth century historians. Access to them was prevented, by the terms of his will, until 1890. The first publication of the Steep Holm material was in *Steep Holm – a case history in the study of evolution*, in 1978. I have repeated it here, with a few changes which have resulted from correcting that copy against the original. Spellings have been left as Skinner had them, apart from modernising his occasional long 's',and are all rather obvious (Burnback = Birnbeck; Pennarth = Penarth; Old Wormices = Ole Worm [1588-1654], the Danish physician and antiquary whose name was Latinised as Olaus Wormius; carrot = Alexanders).

These extracts and plates from John Skinner's manuscript are reproduced by permission of the British Library Board, reference Add. MS 33728, ff 39, 50, 38, 44, 45 (drawings 32, 40, 38, 35, 36):

"26 July 1832 – I rose soon after six, and walked with my daughter to the Bath before breakfast; also engaged a boat for sailing, the wind being more favourable, and Joseph I knew would enjoy another trip. We were obliged to walk to Burnback in order to get into a small boat to convey us to a larger which we had hired to take us to Steep and Flat Holmes.

117

"As it blew briskly, we were not long in reaching the former Island, about seven miles distant from the Bay; while on our course thither I made three sketches, one of the South east side of the Steep Holmes; another of the Flat Holmes, with its Lighthouse, and the Welch Promontory called Pennarth Point beyond: the third was taken as we approached the landing place, of the Steep Holmes, which shows a house now building for an Inn, by Mr Baker, the Proprietor of the Island which he lately purchased for £700, a very cheap bargain, if it be true that he lets the fishery for £40 a year.

"Owing to the carelessness of the man at the helm, we ran on a shingly bank outside the little Harbour, and were obliged to go on shore in the small boat: had it blown hard, the sailing boat we quitted would have been in great danger, as the surf sometimes breaks from 15 to 20 feet high over the bank as we learnt afterwards.

"The man says it never occurred to him before to ground on approaching the Island, as he knows every inch of the shore having been occupied in fishing on it from his youth up. In order to render the little Harbour more secure, a number of men are now actually engaged in building a Pier under the new Inn, which will then be frequented perhaps by the coasters coming up the Channel.

"There are two small huts on the rock, besides this more extensive habitation, both appear to have been recently erected.

"In times past, Gildas, the monk, denominated Badonicus, from having been born at Bath, fixed his solitary residence on this rock where he might have realized the miseries he complains of inflicted by the Saxons on the Britons; but being disturbed in his meditations by the Pirates who sailed to and fro, he removed to Glastonbury. The Danes we find also frequently visited this barren rock, and probably made it a receptacle for their plunder taken on the Welch and English shores, and it was the scene of the sad catastrophe which befel them during the reign of Edward, anno 918 [914,actually], as we learn from the Saxon Chronicle of this year, that a large fleet of the marauders entered the mouth of the Severn, under two leaders, Ohter and Hroald . . . [extract from Chronicle omitted].

"An old man – who inhabits the hut at the summit of the rock, and had resided here seven months for the purpose of clearing away the Privet, and wild carrot [Alexanders] which now almost wholly occupy the surface, and planting the soil thus recovered with potatoes and garden stuff – informed me that while digging within the small inclosure which he calls his garden, he came to a vault or cist, seven feet long by four wide; the walls formed of stone without cement, and covered with flat paving stones as he called them: within was a human skull, and skeleton with skulls of sheep, and other bones, some of which appeared to have been burnt, but there was no appearance of any weapon or vessel."

"On my pointing out similar fragments of pottery to those I had before noticed, which were more abundant in his garden, than in the bank I first examined, he said that he was surprised at the quantities he turned up when digging, and added the people must have been very careless of their ware to break so many pots and pans.

"I noticed tiles and bricks, some of the former hollowed out after the Roman manner; but they might also be attributable to a later period; perhaps they belonged to the small religious house, said to have been established here by one of the Berkeley family which might have occupied the site of the present Cottage.

"I perceived the old man has some cucumbers and cauliflowers in his garden, but complains of the trouble of watering them, as there is only one spring on the Island, and that a small one near the base of the rock, but poor Joseph who felt himself thirsty was very grateful for a supply from the small stream: indeed I endeavoured to dissuade him from climbing the Steep, but he seemed so bent on doing it, that he was not to be deterred either by the heat of the weather, or his own short breathing from accomplishing his object. I made a sketch before we ascended the rock of the little Harbour beneath, and a second from the summit, covered by dwarf privet, and quantities of wild Carrot which they here call, I know not for what reason Alexander: the stalk grows to the height of two or three feet, and bears abundance of seed, the roots of some being nearly the size of my wrist, for want of better fuel I perceived they bind the stalks of this herb into bundles to burn.

"I noticed as I proceeded, where the Privet did not entirely cover the soil, patches of wild Strawberries still bearing fruit, also a plant resembling sage; and in places where there is no depth of earth, a fine herbage covers the rock, supplying food for the rabbits which once abounded here, as well as on the Flat Holmes, but they are now nearly destroyed, since a dog and cat have been admitted as residents by the old man, for he was the [Alexander] Selkirk [prototype for Robinson Crusoe] of the domain till masons were sent over from Weston to build the Inn and the Pier below his elevated habitation.

"While pursuing the track of a narrow footpath to the northern [western, actually] extremity of the rock worn through the dwarf Privet, by the feet of Pilots, who land here to have a good look out on the Channel, I put up a Thrush, a Lark, and a Wheatear; numbers of screaming, or rather laughing Gulls, soared above my head, apparently inquiring my business there, and the waves murmured against the crags beneath.

"During a storm this must be a sublime situation, but I was perfectly satisfied to find it as it was. There seems to have been a wall of loose stones running North and South [west to east, actually] along the dorsum of the rock from the old man's residence towards the centre where it branches off to the right. I also traced some cross walls.

"If the Danes were compelled to sojourn here for any time, they needed some such shelter; if they stowed their plunder here, there was another inducement; or perhaps their officers employed them thus to keep them from murmuring at the privations they were obliged to undergo when the Saxons block-aded the coast.

"At the very extreme point northwards [westwards, in fact] nearly opposite to the Flat Holmes and Pennarth Point on the Welch Coast, I noted an oval outpost or signal station, which I should certainly call a Danish work, having before seen similar remains attributable to this people; it measures within the oval about 20 paces by 18; the walls formed of loose stones might have been about four feet wide, the uprights being fixed in the soil, or rather the rock, and the inner space filled up very similar to the workmanship of the vitrified Forts in Scotland, extending along the height from Inverness almost to the Firth of Clyde.

"Dun Iaarl which I particularly examined, is not much larger than this, being situate on the very apex of a pyramidical hill, well adapted to convey signals by fire. Craig Phadric, nearer to Inverness, is of the same oval form, but nearly as large again as the former. Not far from Danes Hill on Mendip, there is a similar Oval Beacon inclosure which I have sketched.

"As the Danish Pirates so much frequented the Severn, it would be hardly possible for them to have navigated its danger-ous Channel without some such directing Beacons. There might have been a similar one on the Flat Holmes where there is now a Lighthouse, and thus the passage, nearly three miles across, would have been marked out and defended for their night descents on the east side of the coast. The name *Holm* is evi-dently a Danish term, signifying an Island; vide Stockholm; and the family I married into were I presume Islanders, or de Holmes originally. Those of the Isle of Wight evidently were, if they trace so old a pedigree, as do the Oglanders who were established there before the Norman Conquest.

"The sketches I took will best describe the situation of the Beacon and the form of the Island, which is said to be nearly a mile and a half in circuit, nearly of an oval shape resembling a Danish Tumulus, described by Old Wormices [Ole Worm] as a ship turned bottom upwards. When the Privet is grubbed up and the loose stones removed, it is not improbable but weapons or some indicia of its warlike occupiers may be discovered; as Mr Baker the proprietor of the Holm is I find fond of antiquities he will, I dare say, keep a good look out.

"Having finished my observations on the summit, I descended with my son and daughter to the beach, where we witnessed the blasting of the rock above the Pier, with an explosion as loud as a Cannon, but we had no apprehension of the falling fragments, being sheltered by a ridge of projecting rock. While waiting for the boat, I made a sketch of this rock, running in horizontal strata, and apparently containing iron ore.

"Brean Down and the Brent Knoll are conspicuous objects on the opposite shore. As we sailed away, I sketched the southern end of the Holm, shewing the Pier now building, the New Inn, and a hut occupied by the workmen close to the zig zag path of ascent, with that belonging to the old soldier employed to cultivate the soil.

"It blew quite brisk as we returned; we steered to Brean Down, where a fishing boat was trolling, and had caught 34 pairs of Soles, some of which I wished to purchase to send to my mother, but they asked more than she would have got them for at Bath.

"I made two sketches of Brean Down whose name indicates the projection above the line of passage, which as I have before observed was fortified by the Belgic British before the Romans established themselves in these parts, and inclosed a fort near the centre of the Peninsula to guard the mouth of the river, or rather the estuary, as it was in those days, running up as far as Glastonbury. Roman pottery and coins have been found here, and as some of the grassland is about to be turned up by the plough further remains may be brought to light.

"Brean Down forms one arm of West Bay, as Worle Hill does the other, and in the course of years I doubt not the whole of the flat will be gained from the Sea, as was the level ground gained in past times from the Astuary Uxella. I paid the boatman for himself and assistant and boat, half a guinea, and hired them for the following day to take us to the Flat Holmes after breakfast.

Owen and his friend Stewart joined us at dinner, they had taken Wells and Cheddar in their way from Camerton to Weston; the little lecture I had previously given respecting our want of accommodation had a good effect, since they were promised comfortable beds, and in the evening perambulated the place, which was quite new to Owen's friend though not to himself. Joseph was not the worse for his exertions."

27 July 1832 – "I walked with Anna before breakfast to the Bath: afterwards we entered the sailing boat which lay off at anchor head, purposing to reach the Flat Holmes, but the wind dying away, and the tide running strong down Channel, we failed in our purpose, and brought up in a little harbour at the Steep Holmes which we had visited yesterday, but which was quite new to our guest. I took three sketches in Weston Bay; a fourth of the South East side of the Steep Holmes, shewing what is called the Rudder Rock at the northern extremity.

"On landing, I pursued my former path to the Fort or Signal station taking en passant another sketch of the Flat Holmes with its Lighthouse just opposite to the summit of the Island, between two upright rocks forming a natural doorway; and beyond that another memorandum of the Danish Signal post with the path leading to it.

"We returned to the boat before the tide flowed up Channel with the expectation of reaching the Flat Holmes, but the boat-man pretended he could not as the wind then blew, but I was sailor enough to be assured he was purposely imposing on us wishing to hasten our return to Weston that he might get another party on board in the evening, although I had hired the boat for the whole day. I expostulated but to no purpose.

"Going round the west side of the Steep Holmes, I made four sketches, and on our return to Weston, two of the Bay. The boatman pretended to press us to go back to the Flat Holmes saying the wind would then enable him to reach it, and was fair for coming back, but he had heard us say that we had ordered dinner at four and meant to walk in the evening.

"Before I paid him I took an opportunity to say I should not hire his boat again when I came to Weston, and that he ought to remember the old saying, grasp all lose all.

"I walked in the evening with Anna, Owen, and Mr Stewart along the sands to Uphill, and returned so completely tired, I was not sorry to go to bed as soon as I penned in my sketches. Joseph evidently is the better for the air and amusement he has found at Weston, but we all agree it is a wretched place to continue in for any length of time."

OPPOSITE. **Rock-built: Cliff Cottage is set in the side of the eastern cliffs. Seen from the south-east. Photographed by Colin Graham in 1974.**

All in the mind: Rodney Legg contemplating what was left of John Baker's Inn (above, left of centre). Seen from the north-west. Legg's Folly would arise from its rubble and is seen from the south-west. Photographed by Colin Graham in 1974 and Rodney Legg in 1992.

John Baker's Inn

When John Skinner visited the island on 26-27 July 1832, he not only sketched the grandiose three-storey villa on the shore, the Inn, but also the Cliff Cottage on the slope above. Both were unfinished, with the masons working on the buildings and a little harbour beneath the Inn, and the visit was interrupted by blasting which rained down pieces of rock from higher up the cliff.

Skinner's account makes it clear that John Baker, who had "lately purchased" the island for £700, was building the house "for an Inn". This conflicts with later reports that the building was a gentleman's residence that only later became an Inn, and also that it was built by Colonel Charles Kemeys Kemeys-Tynte. Both these errors were perpetuated by me in *Steep Holm – a case history in the study of evolution*.

Stan and Joan Rendell have shown in *Steep Holm: an investigation*, produced in 1977, that John Baker, who lived at Batcombe, near Blagdon, had bought the island, for £700 from William Willes on 24 June 1830, and did indeed erect the earliest part of the Inn – its northern part – along with the sea wall that would later carry its southern extension, and the harbour eastwards from it. He also built the Cliff Cottage and seems to have intended making the island viable from a mixture of managing the fisheries and selling drinks to the Bristol Channel seafarers. There were a multitude of these, in craft of all sizes, and they often had to waste hours in the waters off the Holms whilst waiting for the tide to let them sail into the Welsh ports, or go up to Bristol, or just for the water to come inshore at Weston, Bridgwater and Watchet.

John Skinner's diary also provides evidence that even the Channel pilots stopped by to use the island. It was their path that led across to Rudder Rock where they could see the business that was coming up, and also gain a fairly accurate impression of the next belt of weather.

From the start it seems that John Baker used the opportunities to buy spirits from the seamen and to avoid mainland excise duties. He was not, however, a publican by trade but was a second generation solicitor. The Bakers were leading members of their profession in the area, and John Baker's father had drafted Weston's Inclosure Act of 1810, but the Steep Holm operation seems to have been a drain on their resources. The story in Weston was that an innkeeper from the town took refuge on Steep Holm in the early nineteenth century, for seven years, to avoid arrest for debt. He was said to have ventured back occasionally on a Sunday. This was the folk memory, perhaps, of the demise of John Baker.

He had certainly used the island's extra-parochial status – it is still not part of any civil parish – to avoid a liquor licence, though that was then purely a matter of duties payable to the state rather than the petty constraints which were to be intro- duced much later, by the Defence of the Realm Act of 1916. The island's first Inn was out of business by the end of the 1830s, with the inference being that John Baker had departed, as a visitor recorded in his diary for 30 August 1841 that "just below" the Cliff Cottage " there is a very good house which used to be used for an Inn".

The visitor found the Inn occupied by a fisherman, whose only companion was a boy who occasionally rowed across to help him. Above "the scene was lovely" apart from the derel- iction of Cliff Cottage, which still had its memento of the Peter- loo massacre [at the Manchester Reform Meeting of 16 August 1819]:

"Although it is a good cottage it looked extremely wretched. In the middle of the room was a rude block for a table. At one side of the fireplace a stool with a piece of worn and dirty sheepskin on it by way of a cushion. On the other side a drawer turned up for the boy. In the centre over the fireplace hung a coloured print which seemed to be a Chartist production for it represented an engagement between the people and the mili- tary. And there was an inscription beneath about the Rights of the People, but it was all much defaced. On each side hung fishing tackle, knives and nondescripts of various sorts. The floor was strewn with feathers and bits of decayed fish and the whole was thick with dirt. I wondered how any human being could live in such a place, and worse still in solitude!"

Architecturally, Cliff Cottage is the island's most adventurous building; it is a rectangle with its entire north wall being the cliff- face, rendered with plaster over the living rock. There is one large recess in this wall, having an arched top, and a similar arch above a door. It was the most recently intact of the Steep Holm ruins, still having a sound roof in the 1930s. It had been used as a store for fishing gear up to the winter of 1931, the year when the iron stakes across the shingle spit last carried nets. Cliff Cottage was pulled apart by the army in 1941 as its south-east corner stood directly in the way of an incline railway which was being cut in a series of precise sections along the course of a trackway that had previously meandered to the top of the island.

The next innkeepers would be the Harris family, in 1846, but they would come as tenants. On 1 October 1833 there had been a change of island ownership, from John Baker to the Provincial Grand Master of the Somerset Freemasons, Colonel Charles Kemeys Kemeys-Tynte, who lived at Halswell, near Bridgwater. He paid £2,500. At the time the island was rented to Weston fisherman Benjamin Attwell. The Kemeys-Tynte family held the Wharton baronial title and Steep Holm would remain a part of the Wharton Estate through both periods of military occupation, and until its sale to the Kenneth Allsop Memorial Trust in 1976.

Confirmation that Kemeys-Tynte had indeed bought Steep Holm in the 1830s would come to us from an unexpected source. Denise Levertov, one of the best-known American poetesses, wrote to John Fowles in 12 January 1981 to tell him that her father had bought parts of the Kemeys-Tynte library at Sotheby's after the Anglo-Welsh family died out in the 1930s.

She had found a sepia-wash pencil drawing which had the inscription: "The Steep Holmes an Island in the Bristol Channell (sic). The property of Colonel Tyne M.P." There was also a picture of Rudder Rock, with the following identification: "The Steep Holmes. Wonderfully double arched rocks, they are. I expect you know them."

These pictures, Denise Levertov wrote, were among a myriad of sketches in the two albums that belonged to Colonel Charles Kemeys Kemeys-Tynte and dated from the 1830s. From his boyhood scrawls in other papers she had no doubt that he was the "C.K.T." of the initials. One such was a silhouette of a spaniel: "Duke, a pet dog of my Mother's".

In 1985, Jane Evans of Woodspring Museum came across a short item in the Bristol Mirror of 16 August 1834 that credits Colonel Tynte with what must have been the largest assortment of introduced flora since the time of the monks:

"This island, hitherto considered as a barren rock and mere warren for wild rabbits was lately purchased by Col. Tynte M.P. At present it bears three patches of wheat and one of barley in good state. Also in healthy growth are mangel-wursel, carrots, potatoes, turnips, etc., besides a profusion of wild strawberries, myrtles and geraniums etc. The worthy Colonel sent over in the Spring a large assortment of wild and hedge flowers which are at present in bloom. In a small garden are very fine dahlias and other rich flowers."

The Harris innkeepers

The Harris family arrived on Steep Holm in 1846 and were set to establish the record for the longest island occupancy that has yet been recorded. It would last thirty-nine years.

Frederick Harris senior re-opened the Inn, and with his wife and children carried out subsistence farming, and seemed set to become founder of the island's dynasty. Boats were soon calling again, from both sides of the water, including day excursionists who had found the seaside at Weston-super-Mare which was striving to become a southern spa.

The Cardiff tug *Christine Sinclair* circled the islands on 2 August 1848 in a trip "From Knightstone around the Holms". In the Weston-super-Mare Gazette of 15 July 1850 the sailings are announced of the "favourite new steam yacht" – apparently the 45 ton *Wave* – which was scheduled to make daily excursions "about the Weston Bay, to and around the Steep and Flat Holms, and trips to and from Cardiff every Wednesday and Saturday until further notice".

No woman, however, is an island. The family suffered the sudden loss of daughter Caroline who eloped to marry Abraham Hurman, in Bristol register office, on 14 January 1854. There was also a physical disaster, in about 1860, when a gale swept away the walls of the inn-side harbour and left an unusable jumble of rocks. Somehow the problem must have been overcome, and the beach used instead as it had been in the olden days and is again today, as the Inn was extended. Its southern part, above the squared stones of the 1832 sea-wall which now became its foundations, was added in about 1866-67 when the fortification of the island brought extra custom, navvies, and War Department compensation and mortar.

The steps up the 1832-built sea wall, surmounted by this 1867-added Inn extension, were awash in the easterly swells of May 1989 and had a waist-high indoor tidemark from the storm of 26 February 1990. It was, I thought, a dumb place for the doorstep. Then I read that scientists have confirmed that sea levels are rising at 2.4 mm a year – 16 inches since 1830.

By 1873, island innkeeper Frederick Harris was also the proprietor of a major hotel in Weston-super-Mare, the Royal Claremont Pier Hotel, which claimed to be the only one "in close proximity to the beach, with pleasure grounds and walks down to the beach", and adjoining the new pier on Birnbeck Island. Board and lodgings were from £1 10s per week. He had done well out of the island, its sprat fishery, and the Channel. There his yacht *Mystery* had won races and was usually first with the fish to Bristol market. Harris's advertisements offered "peculiar advantages to visitors and tourists" but these were unspecified – he might have had in mind fresh fish, exhilarating boat rides, or perhaps even the attractions of an island where duty-free liquor might not have been completely unknown.

The Harrises' reign acted out its finale on the mainland, before the Axbridge bench, on 25 August 1884. Magistrates found for Frederick Harris junior, the brother of Caroline, and declared that licensing laws did not apply to Steep Holm because it was not part of Somerset. This was so obviously naive that it had to be reversed and this duly happened, at the Inland Revenue's request, in the Court of Appeal. Henceforth duties were payable. Next year the Harrises departed, via Flat Holm.

In the 1980s, Chris Woodfield of Barry was in conversation with latter-day members of the Harris family, who had returned to South Wales: "The last innkeeper of the Harris line on Steep Holm was Anne Cope Harris. The family then settled in Machen Street, Penarth, where they named their house Steep Holm. That also became a personal name in the case of Beatrice Steepholm Harris.

"Members of the family still recall island stories that have been passed down through the subsequent generations. They were familiar with the Church Cave and speak of Hell's Hole, a pothole on the top of the island. It was said to be bottomless and stones dropped without a sound. There was also said to have been a discovery of skeletons with chains around them. Family mishaps included the inevitable slips and falls, and an uncle slid down a cliff."

Out in the rocks, parallel with the Inn walls, there is an L-shaped line of stones which were the foundations of the small harbour that was swept away in about 1860. Leo Harrison Matthews records it in his 1938 report on the island: "On the beach below the inn can be traced the remains of an artificial harbour, which dried out at low tide. It lies in a natural angle of the rocks which formed two sides of it, and the quay walls had been built out on the east and north sides, the entrance being at the north-east corner. The walls are now entirely demolished, but the line of the foundations can still be traced, and the stump of a wooden pile which stood at one side of the entrance, evidently as a fender, is still in position. The foundations are made of large blocks of stone from the beach. This boat harbour, which would have accommodated small ships up to about 30 or

40 tons, judging by the width of the entrance, is apparently contemporary with the inn, and must have been demolished by the sea not long after its construction."

Past and future: as the old Inn looked (opposite) before the shell of the three-storey building and that of Cliff Cottage (above, right) were blown up by the Royal Engineers, in July 1941, when cutting the incline railway up the cliffs. Seen in the other photograph (above) is an impression of how it might look at the end of the twentieth century, as envisaged by architect and artist Fred Pitfield of Bere Regis in Dorset. Seen from the east in both shots, by J.K. Neale in 1934 and Colin Graham in 1982.

Taking shape: restoration of the former Inn as a wardening depot and for dealing with emergencies on the nearby landing beach. Seen from there (above) from the south-east. Seen from the north-west (below) with Salman Legg running up the path. Seen from the south (opposite) with high tide lapping at the 1832-built sea-wall of the outer corner which supports the remains of the 1867-added extension. Photographed by Rodney Legg in 1991.

Demonstrative: Rodney Legg atop the newly completed east wall of the rebuilt Inn. Seen from the south-west (above) and from the outside, from the north (opposite). In that picture note the old stone cross reset above the upper window and the holes to the left which are intended as stone nesting-boxes for birds. Earlier, when Chris Maslen had constructed the timber 'formers' to support the window arches, it was Salman Legg who was reaching for the sky. Seen from inside, from the south-west (below). Photographed by the Bristol Evening Post and Rodney Legg in 1991-92.

Romantic ruin: John Pitfield photographing the north wall of the long-room of the Farmhouse. Seen from inside the room, from the south. Photographed by Colin Graham in 1983.

Exposition: Betty Allsop (centre) turns away from the fireplace in the west room of the Farmhouse as Rodney Legg (top corner) bores a group of island visitors. Seen from south-east corner of room, from the wall. Photographed by Colin Graham in 1975.

Victorian Farmhouse

I have in front of me as I write the only souvenir, apart from a 1941 Naval, Army and Air Force Institutes mug – since returned – that I have ever taken home from Steep Holm. It is a dark, reddish-grey brick that is stamped "PHILLIPS W-S-MARE"; its gritty texture is superb. This came from the floor of the Farmhouse which stands at the north edge of the stone walled enclosure, covering eight tenths of an acre, on the eastern top of the island. I have also found ridge-tiles stamped "PHILLIPS & SON" and I was surprised that the one which I gave Jane Evans was the first to reach the town collection at Woodspring Museum.

Its wording, Miss Evans explained, dated it to the middle of the nineteenth century. Charles Phillips established his pottery on the north side of Locking Road at Weston in 1847 but his products only carried the family name until 1856. They then called themselves the Royal Potteries and in 1871 the business was sold to John Matthews.

Originally, however, the Farmhouse may have had a thatched roof as the surviving western gable seems to have had its pitch steepened in order to take the tiles. That would put its date to earlier in the nineteenth century but Leo Harrison Matthews, carrying out a survey of the island in 1938, considered that both the building and the enclosure "appear to have been made since the fortifications were constructed in 1867". Harrison Matthews found "some of the grates and a small kitchen stove still in place, as are the wooden door and window jambs. Roofing felt, too, still covers the collapsed roof of a small shed. At one side of the house there is a cemented tank, which is still watertight and filled with rainwater. The enclosure was evidently cultivated as a garden, and lines of stones still show the boundaries of the garden beds. This is not, however, the old garden of the Priory, which is said now to be covered by the Garden Battery."

The documentary evidence is that the Farmhouse was built in 1865. It has survived in something approaching Harrison Matthews's description. In particular the tank still holds water, as Jenny Smith found when she emptied it of rocks in 1979, and its buried treasure was a large sodden model of a Victorian sailing barge. One can imagine the children playing with it in the tank, and their disappointment when it finally absorbed so much water that it dropped into history.

Likewise the building slipped into decay. It is 17.5 metres

long by 5.7 metres wide with a west gable to 4.5 metres in height, plus a metre of chimney, though only in this west room are the walls nearly at their full one storey height. The rest of the building is reduced to 2 metres or less.

Sadly, at the time of writing, the well meaning conservation work of 1976-86 has left it a mess. The 3 metre wide cart-way, midway along the north wall, has been blocked. On the west gable the double roof-line, which showed the development of the building, has been pushed off into obscurity. Elsewhere the walls have been capped by a mound of mortar, oozing over the sides like icing on a Christmas cake, an impediment that will infuriate those who carry out its future rebuilding.

Disappointing also are the field systems that cover the entire island. They radiate westwards from both the Priory and the Farmhouse in a complexity of lines. Certainly that cart-width hole in the Farmhouse wall is matched by a pair of strewn but obviously parallel walls that run from north to south across the top of the island, east of the present Ordnance Survey instrument pillar. Its access point is on the north side, turning eastwards towards what are now the ruins.

All of the many boundaries are now rock piles. I followed and mapped them all in the drought years of 1975-76. The wall that followed the east-west "dorsum" of the island, to borrow John Skinner's word, emerges from beneath the great Victorian stone-heap south of Summit Battery and continues towards Rudder Rock. Another derelict wall, just east from the Barracks, reaches the very edge of the cliff. It is hairy to stand there – the surprise is the amount of Victorian mortar. All the other walls are of dry-stone construction so this one may well have had another purpose, such as holding the military rubbish shute.

The multiplicity of walls enclose fields of half and acre to an acre and a half in size. Jenny Smith and Chris Maslen have picked up pieces of mortaria, bowls for crushing grain, and other Roman pottery in a little enclosed area at the middle of the island immediately east of the eastern of the two parallel banks that I have mentioned. I am sure that it is not a Roman building, however, but a barn for a cart or the stock. Its opening faces the east, towards the Farmhouse, and its size is that of a suburban car-port. Many times, elsewhere in Britain, I have picked up ancient pottery and even carved stones from farm walls. The Roman debris here was probably picked up in the same way, from the fields, and dumped on or beside the nearest convenient wall at the corner of the field. I have walked over enough Roman villas to sense, regretfully, that this is not one.

For all that, the field boundaries sum up the early history of Steep Holm. Part of their interest is that they are inherently impossible to date. Some, perhaps, are Roman. Others may be earlier, and that with the core of mortar is definitely Victorian. Or a Victorian reconstruction! The marvellous thing about the wealth of Steep Holm field boundaries is that they defy dating. It would be both an impossibility and a tragedy to know everything that had happened.

The romance is in not knowing. These field boundaries say this in crumbled stone. They are the evidence that when we think we know everything we shall in fact know very little, and with even less precision. "What date are they?" I asked Ancient Monuments Inspector Beric Morley. "Anything from the Bronze Age to the nineteenth century," he replied. That was a true expert speaking – the only honest answer in life is "don't know". Despite a wealth of facts, and the quarter of a million words that I have inflicted upon it, Steep Holm still retains its mystery.

Cultivation terrace: short length of undated but ancient drystone walling on the southern cliffs, midway between the Barracks and South Landing, discovered by Rodney Legg. Seen from the south-east. Photographed by Colin Graham in 1976.

The end of history: 'Shaan' — Hindi for 'Flame' was a 'Bollywood' Bombay-produced Indian James Bond adventure film, set and partially filmed on Steep Holm and climaxing with the destruction of the Barracks, by blowing up a model created in the studios in Bombay (opposite). Helicopter shots include the northern cliffs from the north-west (above) and the western Victorian barbette and gun barrel at Split Rock Battery, from the north-east (below). The film was made in 1980.

Index